FLUTE

Richard Adeney

Richard Adeney was born in 1920, the son of the painter
Bernard Adeney. He was principal flute with the
London Philharmonic Orchestra for seventeen years, playing with
all the great conductors of the time. He also appeared regularly as
a soloist, and was a member of the Melos Ensemble, the English
Chamber Orchestra and other smaller groups.

He has travelled widely and had a very enjoyable existence,
which he is still seeking to maintain.

flute

Richard Adeney

An autobiography

Brimstone Press

First published in 2009
2nd edition 2009
by Brimstone Press
PO Box 114
Shaftesbury SP7 8XN

www.brimstonepress.co.uk

Designed by Linda Reed and Associates
Shaftesbury SP7 8NE
Email: lindareedassoc@btconnect.com

Printed by Antony Rowe
Chippenham SN14 6LH
www.antonyrowe.co.uk

ISBN 978-1-906385-20-0

All photographs © Richard Adeney except

pp 25 & 27 © Gavin Gordon
pp 42 & 142 © Douglas Whittaker
p 94 © the Celibidache Foundation
p 164 © Emanuel Hurwitz

Permission to reproduce the above is
gratefully acknowledged.

Contents

List of Illustrations

Foreword

In my teens I decided that there were three things that I most wanted from life. They were:

First: That I would become the best flute-player in the world.
Second: To have a huge amount of sex.
Third: To make some sense of the mysterious and confusing world.

This book is an account of how much I succeeded and how much I failed in these three ambitions.

The wish to become a flute player was even more absorbing than my adolescent sexuality, and so the book reflects this and is mostly about music. The third wish, the wish to understand, was intermittent and the weakest of the three, so it isn't mentioned much; and anyway amateurish philosophy, although enjoyable to think and to write, is boring to read.

Myself in 1920

Family

I was born in 1920, early and suddenly, and long ago my mother told me that she'd hardly had time to get onto the bed before I popped out. I'm a rather impatient person, and recently I checked with some musician colleagues, just those I think of as also hasty and impatient, to see if they too had been born early. They had. Did we all decide in the womb that there must be more to life than warm wetness and rumbling stomach sounds, and so choose to get out?

A few days later, I was sitting next to a doctor at supper, and when the general conversation happened to be about early childhood memories I said to him grandly, "I believe that the psychology of the unborn infant, rather than the physiology of the mother, decides the time of birth. I think I, for instance, just got bored and fed-up and decided to be born."

Knowing me well, he said amiably, "Oh come off it, Richard; you really do talk an awful lot of nonsense."

So we checked round the table with people's characters and the length of their time in the womb and no correlation at all was found this time, so the result of my earlier check with my hasty musician friends must have been just hasty chance, just a crackpot theory.

I was named after that crackpot, the painter known early on as Walter Sickert, but later preferring to be called by his second name, Richard. He was a friend of my father but I have no memory of him. My father, who was also a painter, told me that Sickert was a restless man who had four or five studios in North London, painting wherever he chose and sometimes vanishing into a newly rented one where nobody could track him down.

There is a theory that Sickert was the famous Victorian murderer, 'Jack the Ripper' and there are books about this; but the evidence is weak, it seems to me. So, though I'm named after Sickert, I'm *probably* not named after the Ripper.

Sickert was very sociable when young, but in old age was difficult and prickly, known to say jovially to parting guests, "*Do* come again when you have less time;" but when my father knew him he was a famous host and chef, famous especially for his breakfast parties. My father was not only a close friend of his, but also greatly admired his work and he told me that, some years before I was born, they were together in Sickert's Fitzroy Street studio, my father looking at the paintings of Dieppe and Venice standing on easels and hanging on the walls. After chatting about the technique of painting, Sickert said, much to my father's surprise, "Take any one you like."

My father chose only a small, unfinished landscape, and years later he explained to me that he chose it partly because of diffidence, but also because, being a landscape painter himself, he was interested in Sickert's technique as shown in this unfinished picture; he thought he could learn from it. To me, it is uninteresting; what a pity my father didn't take a magnificent vista of the Grand Canal or one of the Bedford Theatre, for it would now be on my sitting-room wall, if I hadn't sold it. I did sell that uninteresting one (which I had inherited later) and that saddened me a little, for I had a sort of family relationship with Sickert. It was like this. My parents were unmarried when I was born, for my father was then still married to the painter Thérèse Lessore; but they soon divorced (so that he could marry my mother) and then *she* married Sickert; so Sickert was my father's wife's husband.

Bernard, my father, fell in love with Noël, my mother, before she had even set eyes on him. It was just after the First World War when Bernard went to a party in Hampstead, and as soon as he came into the room he saw Noël – a sudden dream of loveliness – asleep on a sofa. This is a bit of family lore as told to us, his children; and all continued well, if sometimes stormily, for they were together until Bernard's death forty-six years later.

Bernard Adeney, my father (Photo Noël Adeney)

Although my parents married soon after I was born, I was then illegitimate, for in those days only couples who were *both* unmarried when their child was born were able to legitimise it by marrying; however this law was changed in 1947 and so I then became legitimate, which was not of much interest to me then – or now, for that matter; but I can truthfully say, "I was born a bastard and stopped being a bastard when I was twenty-seven."

In London's Courtauld Gallery, there is a grim-looking portrait of Thérèse by Sickert, but my mother told me that she wasn't grim at all. She behaved extraordinarily mildly at my arrival, a son for her husband, but not for her. Apparently she and Sickert were later happily married, but my father told me that during his first marriage he had had no sex, for on any attempt at penetration Thérèse froze up, became ill and had to be revived; so I wonder how the notoriously sexy old Sickert coped.

In spite of rather frequent squabbles, my parents were well suited and had similar interests. Although Bernard made more noise than Noël when angry, she always won their arguments, so I was astounded and puzzled when I first heard women called 'the weaker sex'; to me, so obviously untrue.

Noël would say, "I'm a yea-sayer", contrasting herself to those dreary people who say no to everything and thus experience little. Bernard was similarly positive, though he wasn't a maker of such pronouncements. They greatly enjoyed life, liked a lot of people, and gossiped vividly about friends.

Another of Noël's sayings about herself was, "I'm a *visual* person." Bernard was too, and indeed they lived through their eyes more than most people, and much of their conversation was about the pleasure and pain of things seen: the wonderful sky that morning, the horror of a neighbour's wallpaper, the delight in finding a pretty chair in a junk shop, discussion of a friend's new sculpture, and so on.

Bernard was apparently dyslexic as a child, but he was remarkably talented at drawing, so when only nine his parents took him away from school and sent him to join the almost adult students of an Art School. As a teenager he became suddenly famous for his large Pre-Raphaelite-style painting of 'Saint Francis and the Birds', the star of the Royal Academy Summer Exhibition of 1897. He taught himself to read in his late teens. In the 1920s and '30s he was still quite well known, but his quiet style of painting couldn't compete with new styles. He was, I think, a very good painter, though his work lacks the impact of, for instance, his contemporary and fellow member of the London Group, Paul Nash; now on the walls of my house, his landscapes have

Noël Adeney, my mother, in her seventies (Photo RA)

a glowing, three-dimensional quality which gives me great pleasure. But one has to know them well to love them. Noël also painted beautifully and her paintings are more striking and colourful than Bernard's, though less carefully designed. My sister, Charlotte, painted well at school (and very well later), so I felt surrounded by talent, but having no talent myself, felt to be the booby of the family.

Noël was the nineteenth of twenty children by her father (and thirteenth of fourteen by her mother). She went to the Slade, where she was a contemporary and friend of Carrington and knew many of the people now known as 'Bloomsbury'. She went to parties at Garsington, had tea with D. H. Lawrence, was punted on the Cam by Rupert Brooke, knew Russell, Keynes, Vanessa Bell and many others. She lived long enough to read the first cult books about Bloomsbury and was often irritated by their factual errors.

She wrote a novel (based on the life of her friend, the writer Denton Welch), designed fabrics for Rodier and made clothes professionally. Her greatest love, though, was painting, and she enjoyed exhibiting, especially with the London Group. She would love to have been a star, and I think resented her lack of success, compensating for this lack by a desire to live other people's lives for them. She was a wonderful listener and an obsessional giver of advice, so her two children came to see themselves as parts of her life rather than as autonomously themselves. Harmful for the children.

I gradually broke free during my teens and twenties and from then on had a guarded and cool relationship with her.

Bernard, my father, in old age became irritable and difficult to get on with, having been jovial in middle age, and only recently have I made a guess as to the cause of this irritability. His whole life, his obsession, was painting, and he spent a great deal of time working at it. When younger he was thought to be among the best of English contemporary painters (I have glowing newspaper criticisms of his solo exhibitions), but later on he faded away from recognition, which must have hurt him deeply.

I very much wish that I'd understood at the time the possible cause of his moodiness, for then I might have been kinder and more forgiving – but I'm afraid that adolescents aren't famous for being either to their parents.

The Tate Gallery has a large portrait by Augustus John of the Portuguese cellist, Suggia, in which she is wearing a magnificent crimson dress which spreads out across the floor. Noël, my mother, made that dress. She told me that actually it was royal blue and that John painted it falsely in the more striking crimson. He was enormously famous as a painter then, and was even more famous as a father of numerous children by numerous women. (Many years later, I lived near Soho and used to see him there. This famous old man was by then very dirty and drunk, and tottered around mumblingly asking young men to have sex with him, who then just told him to fuck off.)

From just before my birth until I was eighteen (that is, from just after the First World War until just before the Second) we lived in a large 1840s house in Haverstock Hill, north-west London. Before I was born, my parents got a lease on it for no down-payment and no ground-rent, just signing an agreement to keep it in good repair. Eton College, the landlords, in under-populated 1919 London feared that their houses would rot and fall down, so they gave them away to people 'of good social standing' (those who had some money and an upper-class accent).

It was a pleasant, airy house, with a large garden for children to play in and a wooden studio where my father painted. Inside, the studio had the sweet smell of turpentine and the acrid one of anthracite from the black stove; and even now, if I smell those smells again, I return to the great untidy room, its walls covered with my father's paintings, with reproductions of Titian and Raphael squared up with ruled lines for design analysis, and remember being shooed out and to leave him in peace. The studio had just a skylight; the lack of windows, and my exclusion while he painted, made it a mysterious and exciting place.

With £800 a year, my family was comfortably well off, though in the 1929 recession the bull-nosed Morris had to be sold; but we kept on our second house in the country and still had servants, one living in to look after the two children and a full-time daily cook-cleaner.

I went to four schools and a music college.

First, six years of hell at a 'prep-school' in St John's Wood. There, the endless boredom of the meaningless lessons, the imprisonment of the classrooms, sadly staring out of the window just waiting for the days to be over, were a bleak horror. But I made friends and even liked some of the teachers, not quite all seen by me as boring and grotesquely ugly.

That experience taught me two things; first, to avoid all education (something I have only recently unlearnt), and, second, to be stoical when painfully bored, which later on helped me through orchestral rehearsals with incompetent, jabbering conductors.

There was almost no music at this expensive school, but at home there was an acoustic, wind-up gramophone, but few records; the one which I remember best, and which I played often, was of the first two movements of Schubert's B flat Piano Trio, with Thibaud, Cortot and Casals. When listening to it I had no visual image of instruments or of people making music; to me, it was just a hugely affecting sound coming from a machine, so, a little later on when I saw it being played, I was astonished to see instruments and players moving to the sounds which I knew so well.

This early hearing of Schubert partly explains why listening to late Schubert now (the G major Quartet, the String Quintet, the late piano music and so on) puts me into a similar trance-like state, and, as in times of extreme panic or overwhelming happiness, I find that my watching, recording self, and my awareness of the rest of the world disappear. I live only in the blissful experience of the music; and this happened strongly with that long-ago listening to the Schubert Trio.

In writing this, I see how my memories are transposed into the minor key of old age, and I tend to forget the jollities of childhood, but however, at home in the evenings, there were games for children and adults together. Charades were highly organised for the large number of people who were usually in the house, and complicated drawing and painting games were carried on at a high standard, my parents urging people on, laughing, encouraging, jeering, hissing, booing, with no self-consciousness. They both had an easy, lively charm which I learnt from them, and (though I may be mistaken about this) people, even now in my old age, tend to like me on first acquaintance, including those who later find me dull.

I also learnt about easy manners from my school-friend Michael, a very well-behaved boy. He and my other best friend never met each other, for

Michael was at school and I saw Shelley only in the holidays. They were both perfect, and never again have I been totally uncritical of people I know well. Michael, a handsome boy with bright red hair, was best at everything at school: he could act, play games superbly, pass exams, and tell hilarious jokes and stories. He always had, it seemed to me, total self-confidence and was never in awe of grown-ups. His mother by adoption had an old house in a pretty village in Essex called Ugley and, like Michael, the house and village were total perfection. Staying there for a weekend, we walked in lanes with sweet-smelling wild roses in the hedges, and in fields where there were friendly horses and donkeys, then returned to an out-of-doors tea with the grown-ups, sitting quietly, eating scones and eclairs. On the lawn of the perfectly-kept garden, surrounded by Sweet Williams and peonies, I felt I had to behave perfectly, but, never having seen an eclair before, I bit hard into mine and splattered cream down my shirt-front, causing red-faced humiliation.

My holiday friend, Shelley, was wise and serious. He knew about horoscopes and Buddhism and the evil of eating meat. Aged eleven, we went on an all-day outing on our bicycles, taking lunch with us, the longest time that I had ever been away without adults. We rode first on flat main roads where cars were still rare, away from the Sussex coast near Chichester, and on up into the Downs to Goodwood. We ate our delicious sandwiches on the hard, rabbit-cropped grass among the dried, clean pellets of their dung, surrounded by little blue and yellow flowers and the strong smell of wild thyme. Afterwards, having survived a perilous and rapid descent of a great hill, not using my brakes because Shelley was brave enough not to, we arrived home, exhausted, feeling as though we'd explored the Borneo jungle.

Sir Henry Royce lived nearby. When Shelley and I were walking along a narrow track back from the beach, we saw him from way off, driving towards us in his superb, pale-blue, open-topped Rolls. Shelley picked up a large, sharp ploughshare and put it in the way of the car, and we watched from behind a hedge with dread and excitement, thinking of a burst tyre or a broken axle, but Sir Henry, his handsome, white-bearded face looking serene, calmly drove over it, aware of the ground clearance of the car from his own factory.

On growing up I lost touch with my two great friends, though I know that Shelley became a sculptor and was for a time an assistant to Henry Moore.

I knew Moore at the same time as I knew Shelley, though they didn't know each other then. This was in 1932 when my family and I, then aged twelve, went on holiday to the Suffolk coast. That year, Moore, a friend of my parents, was staying near by; he is the man looking into the camera in the photograph which has our motor caravan in the background. He was already known as an abstract sculptor, and my parents were amused at seeing him wandering along Dunwich beach, entranced by the odd-shaped pebbles that he found; they jokingly said he was going to copy them. The beach was sinking and above it were collapsing cliffs and a graveyard; human bones fell and mingled with the

Bernard Adeney, Henry Moore, Charlotte (my sister) and Mrs Moore in 1932. The motor caravan is in the background. (Photo Noël Adeney)

pebbles, giving Moore further samples. He was a fine swimmer, doing a stylish crawl, and I admired his beautifully shaped body; he wore only a tiny jock-strap, not the usual large body-covering bathing costume of the time, which was exciting. He would swim far out into the rough sea, into its well-known dangerous currents, and I felt anxious when he was so far away, a little dot far beyond the huge, hostile waves breaking onto the shingle, and at night he even swam out through the shining moonlit phosphorescence, his head sparkling in the darkness until he almost disappeared.

Schools

My family seldom went to concerts, and the first one I was taken to was a violin recital in a village hall in Sussex. It was horrible. I found the violinist's sound bearable though uninteresting when she played on one string, but when she used two at once I was in acute pain, putting my fingers in my ears, dreading the next time the terrible scraping sound would happen. Even now I tend to feel uncomfortable at the sound of violin double-stopping, perhaps because of that early horror.

The next concert I went to was also horrible. It was in London this time, an orchestral concert for children. For most of it I heroically kept silent in spite of having a tickling cough, feeling that my lungs would burst in the effort. Malcolm Sargent conducted and he also talked about the music, but, even when at last the itch in my throat stopped, I got no meaning from his words – a foretaste of future boredom with conductors, perhaps?

That autumn, I didn't return to the unpleasant prep school but was sent instead to King Alfred's, a civilised school in north London, where I still managed to avoid being educated, but did learn how to make recorder-like instruments out of bamboo. This became an obsession and I spent hours each day cutting their finger-holes to tune them and changing the shape of their embouchures to make them sound sweet. The usual tensions of family life and worries about growing up disappeared when I played – and at last I'd found something I could do well.

My parents were encouraging and never showed irritation at the noise. A tune that I played obsessionally, and which they must have got terribly fed up with, was Purcell's 'I attempt from love's sickness to fly'. Only recently have I come to understand why these words fitted my feelings so well then.

Soon after that I went to hear an amateur orchestra rehearsing in a large barn in Essex. It took place at what is called a 'Music Camp', where people get together in the summer to play music and live communally, events that still happen. As I came in and heard the sound of the orchestra, I was suddenly and unexpectedly overwhelmed by emotion, in the same way as I would be overwhelmed by the Marcel Moyse record a year or so later at Bryanston School. I have no idea now what music was being played; all I knew was the flood of my reaction, feeling that I was expanding out of my body to be united with this wonderful orchestral sound. The glory of it stayed with me for days and I even wondered whether I would ever one day be able to join in making these sounds myself. But I played only my bamboo pipes, so that prospect seemed unlikely.

At Bryanston, my next school, however, there was an orchestra and music teachers. Using a battered old school instrument, I had flute lessons from a local bandmaster who taught anyone at the school who wanted to learn a wind instrument. On first holding the flute I thought, "This is my future," and looked at it with awe, then spent hours by myself working out how the complicated keys worked. But at first I disliked the sound I made, for it was thick, breathy and dull compared to the sweet-sounding bamboo instruments which I'd made myself; but I saw that the flute was more serious, an advance, and forced myself not to play my bamboo pipes ever again, though for a time they were a hard-to-resist temptation and I would sometimes hold them lovingly, but never lift them to my lips.

Each day, after lunch, there was a time when all the boys had to listen to classical records. We took small mattresses to the huge, ornate school hall and lie down, forced to rest and listen to music coming from the speakers on the walls. In contrast to the noisy hassle of school life, I enjoyed quietly lying there with the tranquil sounds washing over me.

One day, expecting just another ordinary, pleasant record, there was one that was quite different; it was of Marcel Moyse playing a Mozart flute concerto, and I was overwhelmed. The music hit me like a physical assault that went to the pit of my stomach, not to my ears, and I was no longer aware of where I was but lay, crying without shame, ignoring the other boys.

Afterwards, having packed away my mattress, I walked alone in the sunshine towards the playing fields, with Mozart still singing in my head in vivid bursts of sound that again made me cry. I felt expanded, bigger than my body, and floated along as if not touching the ground. The trees I walked under had head-high upward bends in their boughs, especially shaped for me to pass under them, and the gate into the meadow was open, waiting; the whole world was perfect. Moyse had so shaken me that even my kidneys must have reacted, for I had to stop several times to pee, producing an enormous amount of urine.

That evening, I wrote to my parents, asking them to buy the record and, when at last I got home for the holidays, I greeted no one, found the record, told my family to leave me alone, and played it.

Moyse was again overwhelming – and he'd set the course of my life.

I practiced a lot and the day came for my first rehearsal with the school orchestra. We played Schubert's Unfinished, which was impossibly difficult, especially the syncopated notes; it seemed that everyone else was playing perfectly and I was the only one struggling. Nevertheless, being in the middle of an orchestra was perfect happiness, something quite unlike everyday life, and I lived through classes, through games, waiting between the weekly rehearsals, longing for the next one.

Already, in 1934, only a year after Hitler became Chancellor, there were Jewish German boys at the school, presumably the sons of intelligent parents who had seen what was coming. These boys were different in my eyes from the others at the school because they accepted the enjoyment of classical music as a normal part of life, and they talked to me about it in a matter-of-fact way that told me a lot. One of these fourteen-year-olds told me how he prepared himself mentally for a concert, settling himself into a receptive mood. For them, as there was for me, there was more to life than lessons and games.

Bryanston then had an obsessional policy of physical exercise for the boys. Before breakfast, wearing shorts in whatever weather, we had to run down a mile-long drive and back again, then plunge into a cold bath (perhaps the tenth or twelfth boy into, by then, very dirty water). Mid-morning, there were outdoor exercises, and all afternoon there were games. I think the idea was to exhaust us so that we had no energy left for masturbating ourselves or each other. Adolescent sexuality isn't so easily stifled, but I was so exhausted by this routine that I needed most of all to rest, and the lessons and the after-lunch record sessions were the only time for that. So, as at my previous schools, I learnt almost nothing.

My next and last school was Dartington, in Devon, in beautiful countryside, where the teachers and the other children made the school comfortable and home-like. It was co-educational, and I found its placid heterosexual atmosphere less worrying than one-gender Bryanston's over-exciting homosexuality. But, all the same, I was often unhappy at home as well as at school, for by then I had for many years been desperately worried about my own homosexuality, which caused frequent depressions (along with happy times when able to ignore the worry). Thinking of myself as a tragic outcast, I used flute-playing as an outlet for anguish about my 'love's sickness', as it seemed then, echoing the Purcell tune that I had played so often on my bamboo pipes. Playing was weeping. Looking back now in old age, I find it hard to understand why I was so very depressed for so many years. Why didn't I realise then that homosexuality, even at that repressive time, was something I would cope with comfortably later on?

From about the age of six I'd had worrying, compulsive thoughts about boy's and men's bodies, and believed that when at last I was nine years old, and therefore grownup, this would stop. (It was a family joke that when my father told stories of his childhood he always began with, "When I was a boy of nine...," so, as I couldn't imagine him ever being a child, 'nine' meant 'grownup' to me.) I waited impatiently day by day for my ninth birthday and the longed-for cool adulthood, and when at last the birthday arrived I was devastated at the lack of change. I spoilt my birthday supper with a sulking silent depression and was sent early to bed – where I returned to the unabated, guilt-ridden sexual fantasies.

These fantasies were strange. One, repeatedly, was that I was walking across a field in which there was a flight of steps down into the ground. I took these steps to a door which was opened by a man who showed me around an underground circular room. Around its edges were many naked men chained to the wall, and I was allowed to touch their penises.

Another fantasy, perhaps even stranger and also many times repeated, was that I was walking alone on a deserted beach and on the sand I came across a drowned man. I then undid the trouser buttons of this corpse and felt its penis. These were the night-time thoughts of the little boy wearing a beret looking out from the car in the photograph opposite this page.

At eight I thought of a way by which I could fondle a real live penis. At school there was a red-haired boy called Ian, also eight. I didn't like him much, but I realised that if he came to stay the weekend with me, then we would share a bedroom, though not a bed, and that in privacy I would be able to get into his bed. And, importantly, I chose Ian because I guessed that he was a boy who would co-operate, though nothing had happened either by word or deed between us to suggest this. I fixed it all up by asking my mother and his mother. He came to stay and it worked out exactly as planned. Very exciting for both of us.

Not until my teens did this penis fetishism begin to develop into homosexuality. As evidence for this change, I possess now a clay-modelled man's head that I made when I was thirteen. I modelled this as my ideal of sexual attractiveness – not, of course, telling anyone *why* I was making it – and feeling deliciously guilty while doing so. That I was then interested in a person shows that I was progressing a bit from my earlier interest only in penises. But I must say that what I thought of as my 'ideal man' seems rather strange now.

This slight maturing of my sexuality didn't cheer me up. At that age I thought seriously of suicide and planned to jump the next time I happened to be on a high building. But, typical of the low initiative of the depressed, I then thought, "I could, I suppose, go and find a high building, but I'm too worthless to spend so much effort on." A few days later, during an exciting school tour of the Bryant & May match

Noël at the wheel of the 1925 Morris. I have my arm on the ledge.

factory in London's East End, we were standing on a high balcony, so I thought, "Now's the time" – but then decided that I wanted to see the rest of the factory, so another time would be better.

I believed when young that if I tried hard enough, prayed hard enough, tried again even harder, I could change my sexuality; but now realise that this simply can't be done.

During a holiday, about a year after not jumping from the top of the factory, I was walking alone across a field back from the beach towards our house in West Wittering. I reached a stile and stopped, leant against it and did some serious thinking about my future. On the one hand,

The model head of an 'ideal man'

partly because of my failure at school lessons, I realised that I was stupid, and thus not capable of doing any intellectual or interesting work; but, on the other, I felt I had an inner seriousness which most other boys of my age didn't have; a dark, emotional side which must have expression.

18

It was the first time I'd seriously thought about anything. I then wondered whether it might be possible to earn my living as a musician. I saw how well music would suit me; it needed little intelligence, yet it was serious and emotional. This thought was too close to me for discussion about it with anybody – deepest thoughts were private then – so for years I didn't dare ask anyone if playing the flute could be a profession, though I picked up exciting hints now and then.

At fifteen, I had some good lessons from John Francis, a successful flute-player at that time, and he got me my first flute, a wooden Rudall Carte. It quickly seemed to come alive and became part of me, much more so than the unresponsive school instrument. I became conceited about my playing (to compensate, I expect, for my feeling of inferiority as a sexual oddity and as a fool) and was nearly always contemptuous of how my teachers played. How irritating I must have been at this time, though I don't remember anyone showing irritation, so perhaps I managed to hide the contempt.

Later on I also had lessons from several other people, and the only one whose playing I liked was Frank Butterworth, who had learnt in Paris and played in what was then called the 'French Style', which meant using vibrato on a silver flute, rather than no vibrato on a wooden one. Before my first lesson with him, I thought it absurd that my parents had said that I should have more flute lessons, for after all, I thought in my pride, I play perfectly and no improvement is possible. Butterworth cut me down to size and got me practising; in fact, I practised for such long hours that my left arm locked into a flute-playing position and had to be exercised daily to slowly straighten it again.

Unlike Butterworth, most English players then would have been delighted if fortissimo trumpets had sounded from their flutes, for they were always trying to sound louder and thicker. I liked then (and like now) the flute to sound sweet, gentle, peaceful. I remembered the Marcel Moyse records and my sweet-sounding bamboo pipes and compared them to the trumpet-sounding flute-players who later tried to teach *me*, who criticised *me*, their arrogant little pupil, who was also secretly so sad when not playing.

But some adults did make me feel better, and on one occasion Henry Moore gave me encouragement when he came to supper at our house. My parents' parties were big occasions: the polished dining table, the newly polished brass candlesticks and the shining silver, the smell of Chanel, my mother wearing an evening dress and long, green-jade earrings. There was adult talk which I dared not join in, but silently listened to. Moore was one of those rare people who treat children as their equals, and so I liked him very much. During supper, there was a musical discussion.

Moore turned to me, saying, "Richard, you are the only musician here, tell us what *you* think about this."

Then, a big step towards growing up, I haltingly gave my opinion, proud that I was being treated as an adult and a musician and being listened to seriously. Children, even of college age as I was then, see adults outside their families as objects either to avoid or to manipulate, not as feeling creatures like themselves; but Moore's kindness briefly altered that.

At about this time I met another Moore, the eminent philosopher, G. E. Moore, who so much influenced the Bloomsbury intellectuals. At school, I was friendly with his son, who asked another fifteen-year-old and me to stay with his family in Cambridge. During this holiday in the Moores' house, we spent a lot of time listening to the newest records of Duke Ellington, Nat Gonella, Roy Fox and Fats Waller, making a statement of young superiority over our old-fashioned elders; but it was a *mezzo-piano* statement, for the wind-up gramophone had a gentle little sound, quite unlike the sound-systems with which today's youth asserts itself so effectively.

Moore was a quiet and seemingly timid little man, but his wife was a large, pipe-smoking, frightening woman who organised everyone around her. We, the two visiting children, were sorry for him, for he seemed so sad and bullied, and we decided to be extra nice to him, two fifteen-year-olds being condescendingly kind to one of the foremost intellectuals of the early twentieth century.

RCM

At seventeen I went to the Royal College of Music in London and was taught there by Robert Murchie, the first flute of the BBC Symphony Orchestra. Small, paunchy and red-faced, he wore a pale-grey trilby hat, a pale-grey waistcoat under his black jacket, and a carnation in his button-hole. A little strutting man, he stamped his gold-topped cane on the ground as he walked. He was likeable in the afternoons when drunk, but unpleasant when sober in the mornings; but his sober lessons were best, more critical even if not very informative. I hated the sound he made on the flute and thus silently rejected his teaching, which was childishly silly and vain of me, especially as he was so kind to me.

He once asked me to a broadcast in which he was playing at the Maida Vale studios and said that I should be there at eight o'clock, so I arrived at eight in the morning, twelve hours early, and found the studios closed. Back home, too ashamed to admit that I had made such a silly mistake, I pretended to my family that I had heard the broadcast, and then couldn't say that I was going back at eight in the evening. To hide my mistake from Murchie, I invented an inadequate excuse, which he must have seen through, and he never again asked me to a performance. How complicated adolescents are. Why on earth couldn't I have admitted my error and laughed at myself, as I would now?

Also in Maida Vale, during a rehearsal a year or two later, Toscanini asked Murchie to play a phrase in a way that he disliked; Murchie objected angrily when Toscanini insisted, and drunkenly shouted back, "I won't take this from a bloody wop." The BBC sacked him on the spot. (During the First World War he had been in a hard-drinking Canadian regiment in Italy, which explains his addiction to whiskey and

Bernard, Noël, Charlotte, Polly Church and myself, 1937 (Photo RA)

his antipathy to Italians.) He almost never worked again, though he wasn't old. (But a few years later he did play second flute to my first in Verdi's Requiem when I was still very young. I was embarrassed at his being there, my recent teacher, and annoyed that he played too loudly and told him so, being totally insensitive to his humiliation at our reversal of roles.)

The College taught general music, as well as instrumental playing, but, at that time being intolerant of boredom, I avoided it and never learnt even how to harmonise a hymn tune; but I had to take up a second instrument, for it was a rule of the College. I chose the viola, and at the end of the first term there was an exam for 'second study' instruments.

Before going into the room to play, I chatted to the exam accompanist, a stranger to me.

"You know," I said, "I really can't play the viola at all."

After we'd played, he came out laughing, and said, "And I thought you'd been joking!"

Playing the flute in the College orchestras was for me the best of College, though it didn't happen nearly often enough, for orchestral playing was what I wanted to do more than anything, my only ambition.

One day, on the way to rehearsal, I fell down the steps into the hall, badly spraining my ankle. Other students got me to my feet.

"I'm perfectly all right," I said, "just help me get to the orchestra," and I hopped there.

The rehearsal was so important that I ignored the pain then, only later going to a doctor (which reminds me – after more than half a century I still owe Peggy Shiffner, an oboe student, the fee for her doctor, to whom she kindly took me. Peggy, if you read this, please apply to me for repayment. No, I take that back. What would sixty year's inflation and interest be on, say, three guineas? I probably couldn't afford it).

College life was sociable and easy-going. Although generally lazy, I worked hard to improve my flute-playing, and it seemed to me that I was getting on well, so it was deeply upsetting, when I was eighteen, that Robert Murchie and the Director of the College wrote to my parents to tell them that I had little talent for the flute and could never make a living at it. My parents were told that I should abandon music and try some other profession. (By chance, at that time I passed a busking flute-player at South Kensington station, who, on seeing my flute case and guessing that I was a College student, shouted, "You'll never make a living at that, mate".)

There was a family conference.

"Well," I said to my parents, "I may not be very good at the flute, but there's nothing else I can do at all, and I've never passed any exams, so I'll just have to go on trying."

They were doubtful.

"And anyway, if some players I know can make a living," and I named them, "well, so can I."

After some consultation between the College and my parents, Gordon Walker, the principal flute of the LSO, was asked to give a second opinion on my playing. I played to him in a room at the College, and a few days later went to his house. He was kind and helpful and gave me a lesson lasting the whole afternoon, afterwards refusing payment. I was having difficulty with control of the top notes and no one had told me how to alter pitch in order to keep in tune with other instruments and how not to go flat on diminuendos, basic techniques of flute playing. In that one lesson, I was given ideas for practice for the rest of my playing life, and from then on did sound-quality and pitch-control exercises for hours each day (and was turned out of my lodgings for annoying the neighbours). With Walker's recommendation, to my great relief I was allowed to stay on at College.

My warm and generous parents were encouraging and appreciative of my playing, my mother cajoling me into practising whenever I was despondent or lazy. She revered artists, seeing them as superior to other people; and a flute player was more or less an artist, so I was made to feel that working towards being a musician was respectable, whereas working towards a position in a bank or the Stock Exchange would not have been. My parents came to concerts I played in at college, when I was able to show them that my playing was improving.

Years later, colleagues often said to me, "You play so naturally. Lucky chap, it must have come so easily to you." But it hadn't been at all easy. It had been a lot of hard work, and hours of practising.

Sometimes I was sent by the College to unpaid concerts away from London, and I was one of a group of students who went to Dorking to play Bach's Saint Matthew Passion, conducted by Ralph Vaughan Williams. My first engagement. The Bach must have been a bit odd, as, for instance, VW used eight flutes instead of the four that Bach asks for and he substituted violas for the cors anglais, and the large orchestra

Ralph Vaughan Williams. Drawing by Gavin Gordon.

and huge chorus used then wouldn't be thought correct nowadays; but to me it was tremendous, glorious, overwhelming, and seemed a foretaste of happiness for ever.

Vaughan Williams, a pleasant-mannered and much-liked man, taught composition at the College. He was said to be very stimulating, especially by his prettier girl students, who had to keep well away from his roving hands. They saw this as a mildly amusing joke, not with the outraged indignation which would be the case now in our in some ways more puritanical time.

At the College the orchestras' conductors were Malcolm Sargent (about whom I'll make many jokes later), Constant Lambert, and the College Director, George Dyson. Of these, Lambert was the most interesting. Dyson had the cheek to use the students to try out his own new compositions, which in fact were adequate for orchestral training and were enjoyable, with many wind solos; even then, unlike most of the other students, I wasn't embarrassed to shine in orchestral solos. Even during adolescence I usually felt comfortable in front of audiences, for I was by then used to feeling self-conscious; when going into a room full of people I felt that all eyes were on me, and even walking along a London street I would glance compulsively at my reflection in shop windows, not from vanity but from fear that I was looking ridiculous to all those strangers I imagined were looking at me. So, in front of a concert audience, when people *really* were looking at me, was no more worrying than everyday life, when I imagined they were.

Since a terrifying concert at College with Malcolm Sargent conducting, I have always been scared of playing the piccolo. The College orchestra played Scheherazade in its end-of-term concert and I played the piccolo part very badly. I was so paralysed by nerves on this great occasion, and played so tentatively, that I made a feeble little sound, well below the pitch of the orchestra. I knew I was playing flat. Sargent gestured at me over and over again to blow into the instrument to warm it up, for a warmer instrument is a higher-pitched one; but I just sat there, pretending not to see him, looking down at my knees and feeling that the end of the world had come, or at least the end of my unstarted career. Each

Malcolm Sargent. Drawing by Gavin Gordon.

piccolo entry was flatter than the last and, sitting high up on the College platform, I thought the whole audience was glaring at me.

After the concert, the orchestra filed out past Sargent, and as the clarinettist, Sydney Fell, passed, he said to him, "Bravo my boy, you will go far".

To me, he said, harshly, "You must learn to warm up that instrument; it sounded appalling." The depression following this concert ruined the summer holiday that followed, for I spent it miserably moping.

Next term, when playing the flute with the College orchestra (thankfully, not the piccolo this time), Sargent thought that my playing was too cool and detached. He commented on this saying, "You must identify yourself with the flute; *be* the flute."

I objected, and said to him across the orchestra, "But I'm not a flute; I'm a flute-player," and the other students laughed. Even though my reply was so silly, I felt quite a hero at having cheekily answered the great Malcolm Sargent, for I was already growing into the touchy, bolshy, down-to-earth tradition of English orchestral musicians.

But, in spite of Sargent, I hugely enjoyed the music at College, the chamber music and solos, and especially the orchestra. Flute-playing was as blissful as ever and I noticed that I was more emotionally involved with playing than most of the other students, for many played as if doing a task to be done correctly, not feeling anything.

We were left to organise our own playing of solos and chamber music, and a few of us organised concerts with any player we admired. An admired student was Maria Donska, who was older than most of us and had already studied with Artur Schnabel in Berlin. Although I'd never spoken to her, I'd heard her play Brahms's Second Piano Concerto excellently with the College orchestra, and I plucked up courage and asked her to play Schubert's variations for flute and piano with me. To my surprise and pleasure she agreed to my cheeky suggestion and we worked together on this difficult piece at her house in St John's Wood, and eventually we played it in a concert at College.

She talked about music in a warm and intelligent way that I hadn't come across before. To me at this time, music was music and words

Maria Donska (Photo RA)

were words, and I had no idea that one could mix the two and talk about rubato, musical form, the reason for choosing a tempo and the historical roots of a piece of music. As with her teacher, Schnabel, she had thought deeply about music and, although her playing was emotional and serious, it lacked surface prettiness. She played Chopin and Weber with little rubato, which was thought dull then, but her most intense playing was of Beethoven. At the end of one of our rehearsals she played to me the whole of the Appassionata Sonata, which amazed me. As her style was unfashionable and as she had recur-ring bouts of illness, she didn't have great success in her career. We remained friends until she died in her eighties.

Another student who became a life-long colleague was Cecil Aronowitz. He first played the violin, but his large hands swamped it and he soon changed to the viola.

When people from widely differing cultures meet, each may see the other as simple-minded. Imagine an immensely skilful Kalahari Bushman meeting a Wall Street stock dealer, or a Japanese electronics expert meeting a street-wise London dustman, each of them seeing only the other's ignorance of what they see as really important: that is how Cecil and I saw each other. He was a South African with Lithuanian-Jewish parents, and because we had such different back-grounds I thought him a simple, ignorant fellow, not worth taking seri-ously; not until years later did I realise that he thought the same of me. But, as colleagues, we were happy together, though I found him too opinionated about music and he found me too slapdash.

He always signed his name Cecil <u>S.</u> Aronowitz, strongly underlining the S. He refused to tell me what it stood for. Years later, I peeped at his passport and saw that it was Solomon, but I don't know whether he was underlining his wisdom or his being Jewish, for we never talked about anything personal, only about music or musical gossip.

Already, at College, he was always busy, always in a hurry, and, if he was not rushed, he was depressed. Because I expressed my unhappiness about my sexuality by playing warmly, I thought that his emotional playing showed that he too was worried and unhappy, but, if this was so, I didn't find out why.

He was eccentric and, I thought, a show-off, but his eccentricities were mild. He surrounded himself with teenage girls, whom he called his daughters; he liked jam with all food, even fish; he owned cars which, he said, went without ever needing petrol; he played a third-rate viola, insisting that it was the only one he could manage; and he had a smelly cat he called Tinkerbell, but which others called Stinkerbell.

With no ambition for fame and no interest in money, and thus no feeling of rivalry with other musicians, he had a continuous kindness

Cecil Aronowitz (Photo RA)

and sweetness of temperament. All through his life he showed the warm emotion of music; music was his obsession – and he added to my happiness in music for forty-five years. He died suddenly when playing a Mozart string quintet, his most-loved music, in the Snape Maltings, his most-loved hall.

In 1938 (I'm now back to my College days), the *Daily Mirror*, or some other tabloid, ran a front-page story, with a huge headline, about the disappearance of a seventeen-year-old student from the Royal College of Music. This was followed a few days later by a story of this student being found in a sailors' club in Plymouth, playing the trumpet in the band; then the next day we read that the police had brought him back, along with the pretty London girl he'd taken with him. Of course, this was the talk of the College.

Soon afterwards, I was standing in the queue of the College canteen when another student whispered to me that in front of us was the notorious trumpeter, so I got into conversation with him. He was Malcolm Arnold, who, later on, became a well-known composer. He seemed pleased that I'd spoken to him, and this meeting quickly led to friendship.

He was an odd-looking boy; he had a handsome face, but to me he was unattractive-looking because he slouched, head forward like an old man, and turned his feet out, shambling along; but he was full of jokes and jollity and was the most extrovert and daring person I'd ever met. Among my many friends at College, he became the closest, and we were always laughing, arguing hotly, gossiping and wandering around London looking at the sights and talking to strangers in pubs and along the way. With him, everything was a light-hearted joke. I caught from him, like a benevolent virus, a new self-confidence and optimism, both in my playing, which he praised, and when meeting new people.

His family, shoe manufacturers, either took to drink or were excessively respectable and religious (there is a chapel near the family house in Northampton with a small thin spire known as 'Arnold's toothpick'). Those shoe-making families were an odd lot; for instance, the boss of Barratts, a well-known shoe company, benevolently funded the building of a maternity hospital. When it had been built he insisted that he himself was pregnant, and as benefactor had to be given a bed and full antenatal treatment.

Malcolm believed in the glamour of drunkenness and the supremacy of youth; he said he was going to kill himself at thirty, for he had no intention of becoming a dreadful, boring old man. He did become a very gloomy old man, gave up drink and died at the age of eighty four.

In 1939 he was soon the centre of a group of lively students, and the College would have been dull without him; gathering in the College canteen, we all gossiped about music, musicians, and also about the lugubrious, adult teachers whom we thought were an obsolete breed, so much inferior to us brilliant young ones. Although Malcolm was already writing music, his first study was the trumpet, which he played wonderfully well; his composition was light-weight then and I remember only the jolly solo pieces which he wrote for his friends.

He was creative in many ways, so I never knew when to believe his gossip about our fellow students. For instance, was it *really* true, as he said, that the fat, jolly soprano paid the handsome New Zealand violin student for sex? Did the pallid girl who played the viola *really* sell her body on the streets? Had he really been to bed with so *very* many of the girl students? And had he *really* been caught by the police having sex in Hyde Park in full daylight? I wondered what he said about me to our fellow students, for, though I was secretive about it, he must have realised that I was 'queer' and, having no knowledge of the details of my sex life, probably invented them for others' amusement. I did once bring to the College a pretty young Siamese, but I don't think Malcolm saw him, and unhappily the boy soon gave me up for someone else, so he wasn't around with me for long.

Malcolm was compulsively generous with money, as though fearful of appearing mean; always the first in the bar to buy drinks and insisting on paying the full fare of any shared taxi. But, as I also like to appear generous, and as his forceful generosity made me feel mean, I found his behaviour more irritating than admirable.

I stayed at College until June 1940, nearly a year into the war, seeing fellow students disappearing as they were called up for military service. Germany was then overrunning France in what it called its 'blitzkrieg', its 'lightning-flash' war.

That August, Malcolm and a pretty blonde girl violinist and I went to Cornwall for a holiday, much against the wishes of all our parents, for, as Britain seemed just about to be invaded, it was thought that

Hitler's army might cross the Channel in Dorset and cut off the West Country from the rest of England. For some reason that I now forget, we didn't believe this – or maybe we were just plain foolhardy. Privately I thought that Britain's military position was hopeless and that the war would soon be lost, but of course kept quiet about that.

It was delicious to be the only holidaymakers around in that unusually hot and dry summer, most people being either busily involved in the war or sensible enough not to visit Cornwall. Each of us knew that our immediate future was likely to be horrible, but we had no idea about what was actually going to happen, so we walked in the sun on empty roads to empty beaches and swam and laughed in the heat; and at night Malcolm and I took turns to go to the pretty violinist's bed, he, I supposed, with the greater enthusiasm.

That holiday seemed to be the end of our youth, happiness and freedom.

1939

My father had been in the 1914–18 war and he often told me, "Never again, never under *any* circumstances, should we fight another war." My mother had been brought up as a Quaker and so she too was a pacifist influence. Added to this, I have a peaceable nature. So, because of these three causes, I refused my army call-up in 1938, just before the start of the war, and became a 'conscientious objector'. Nowadays, I think I was wrong and should have seen that defeating Hitler was of first importance, moral scruples coming second; sometimes I still feel guilty, especially when I am with any of my many Jewish friends who so narrowly escaped death. But then I was young, typically thinking that I knew everything, and felt I was making a grand protest not only about the horror of war but also about Hitler's violence, even about the violence of the whole world. I was saying "I am standing apart and above this violent world".

In 1939, in the time between my statement of conscientious objection and the forthcoming tribunal, I was, quite correctly, aware of my ignorance of the future. I couldn't have known that Germany would invade Russia, that America would join the war, that chemical weapons wouldn't be used, that the Maginot Line was useless, that there would be war in the Far East, that the atom bomb would be invented. Though I knew about the ill-treatment of Jews in Germany, I couldn't know that the full Holocaust would take place several years in the future. Added to this, Germany was then allied with Russia and most of my friends in their ignorance still admired Russia's Communism, and this alliance confused me.

I knew that the results of winning or losing modern wars were quite unpredictable (for instance, that the First World War, which was supposed to have been 'the war to end war', had instead indirectly brought about the rise of Hitler, and thus the second war), and I saw that the results of winning or losing this second war were also unpredictable. I thought that people were fighting for a result that could not be predicted and was sure only that killing is wrong, and I held onto that sure idea through a haze of doubt. I suffered many months of acute worry, writing thousands of words of my thoughts into a diary (which I destroyed later on).

During this time I was having lunch with Maria Donska (Jewish) and her friend, Baba, in present-day terminology her 'partner' (also Jewish), and a pianist called Jean Layton (whom I write about later on, when she lived in Prague after the war). Over coffee all three questioned me insistently about my pacifism, and finally reduced me to helpless, guilty silence by their strong reasoning. They all stared at me as in the end I sat, dumb. Each of the young women had unusually large eyes, and being surrounded by these six huge, staring, accusing eyes caused in me a feeling of imprisonment and panic. I excused myself somehow, and went home to further doubts – but finally continued in my pacifism.

In the autumn of 1939 I was tried in a court that had been specially set up to judge conscientious objectors, and I didn't have a good case. Quakers and other people who were members of recognised pacifist religious groups were given the most lenient treatment; but people like me, who merely said that killing is wrong, were usually told to join some non-killing part of the army such as the ambulance service, or were even put straight into the ordinary army. But, much to my amazement, I was given 'unconditional exemption'. I can only guess that the person preceding me had irritated the magistrates, so that they gave him an unjustly harsh judgement, and that they felt guilty about this and made themselves feel better by being lenient with me – or maybe they'd just had a good lunch.

I'm still confused about the rights and wrongs of not fighting and, when gloomy, see reasons for it other than the moral ones that I gave at my trial. I think my parents wanted me to refuse to fight because they feared that I would be killed (though they never said that), and they influenced me. And maybe I was just a coward and scared of army life and the risk of death, and maybe my pacifism was just a cover for that cowardice. I simply don't know.

My feelings against war, against violence, against aggression, were all driving forces for flute-playing. It expressed another side of life from the ongoing war, a peaceful, loving side. When playing, I was saying, "Here is something valuable that is not war-like. *This* is how life should be." That may sound fanciful now, but, during the war, playing to audiences weary of violence and longing for peace, something valuable and peaceful really was given in concerts, and a flute played warmly is the most peaceable sound of all.

Musicians tend to be peaceable people, and later on several of my colleagues found they couldn't stand the army. A bass player (a future chairman of the LSO) put his foot under a bus wheel and thus disabled himself. Malcolm Arnold shot himself in the foot and got out of the army on psychiatric grounds. An oboist, who had been my best friend at Bryanston, lived on a diet of Benzedrine and black coffee and very nearly died, and then was discharged from his Guards Regiment because he was so ill. And a viola player in the LPO, my friend Ray Glasspool, feigned madness; Malcolm Arnold, then in the LPO, successfully acted the part of his psychiatric keeper and together they fooled a medical board into thinking that Ray was unfit for the army. During the examination Ray suddenly feigned mania and rushed around the office opening drawers and throwing huge piles of papers out of the window, and so, a very healthy and sane man in his early thirties, he stayed in the LPO throughout the war.

There was one hero. In the performance of Scheherazade (which I mentioned earlier in relation to humiliation and the piccolo), the orchestra's leader was Denis East, a remarkably handsome young man, with black hair and pale eyes, who played his violin solos with great self-confidence. I hardly dared speak to him because of my awe of his beauty, his prowess on the violin, and his being leader of the College orchestra. He was in the Far East during the war, where he was brutally imprisoned by the Japanese, returning to England grey-faced and subdued, never regaining his spirit and glamour.

Soon after the beginning of the war I left the College, and that year the art school where my father taught moved to Northampton, Malcolm Arnold's home town, and my parents rented a house there. Malcolm was living with his parents near by and so we saw a lot of each other. We got up a concert in the local Town Hall, for which he wrote most of the music under various pseudonyms; for instance, his new flute sonata was in the programme as 'Sonate poor flute, par A Youngman' (the word 'pour' being deliberately misspelt). It was rather good and I wonder where it is now – perhaps lying dusty in some Northampton attic. As the local paper had no music critic, I wrote a review for it myself and for a joke I slated the concert, criticising my own playing especially strongly. Friends who had been in the audience read the criticism and were outraged, one even saying that I should sue the paper.

Although there were these jokes, I was still obsessed with the flute and flute-playing. Walking the dreary wartime Northampton streets, I would escape into dreams of playing, of success, of large audiences; and, even more vividly, the flute sound itself would sing in my mind as continuous background fantasy. I practised for hours each day, mostly to improve intonation-control and tone-quality. I worried little about the future, ignored the war and, aged twenty, lived from minute to minute like a child.

One night I was as usual, like a child, deeply asleep. Then suddenly and for no apparent reason I was fully awake and fully alert. I had time to be very much surprised by this and to notice the quietness of the night, when, CRASH, a German bomb exploded. For years I was puzzled how it could have happened that I woke up *before* hearing the bomb-blast. Did I have the ability to foretell the future, even if by only a second or two? What was going on? Only now do I probably have the answer. Perhaps we all have an emergency wake-up system (using primitive parts of the brain) and the noise activated this and bumped me awake; at the same time the sound was separately and slowly processed in my still-sleepy upper brain, and so only then, seconds later, did I actually *hear* the bomb. It was a long time before I got back to sleep from the heart-thumping reaction, and I never found out where the bomb had fallen, even though it must have been quite close and probably killed people.

Early in 1941, I joined a short-lived orchestra in Bournemouth (grandly called the Wessex Philharmonic) run by Reginald Goodall, a mild and pleasant young man. Because he was confused by his devotion to Wagner, he would seditiously talk to us about the glory of Germany and the genius of Hitler, but no one in the orchestra took any notice and he was accepted as just silly and simple-minded. I liked him and enjoyed his musical enthusiasm and he got what music he could out of this orchestra, the first and worst that I ever belonged to.

Later on, at Covent Garden, Goodall became a great trainer of singers, his workroom upstairs being known as Valhalla, but in his Bournemouth days he had no idea how to make a bad orchestra a bit better technically. He would shout and sulk, but he wouldn't tell the second oboe that he was a quarter of a tone flat or get a chord to start together by persistent practice. But, all the same, his concerts were more than routine.

Because of the war, it was hard to get players to come to Bournemouth. For one concert, neither the second or third flutes turned up for Tchaikovsky's Fourth Symphony, so I had to play all three parts, and enjoyed myself jumping from one part to another, trying to play as much as possible. I easily rattled off the piccolo solo in the scherzo (which, later on, I was to hear so often splutteringly misplayed from two places down to my right), for nobody had told me that it was supposed to be difficult.

The orchestra didn't work hard and, during the hot summer weather, I spent my time off cycling along by the sea, stopping to bathe and sunbathe happily. Having no money for papers or a radio, I was briefly insulated from a world in acute crisis. Although my bed and breakfast in Bournemouth cost only fifteen shillings a week, the orchestra paid so little that I was short of food, but too vain to ask my parents for money. I would sometimes hungrily have a bun and a cup of coffee in a cheap snack-bar by the sea, unable to pay for more, and always the same unknown, sad music was playing there on the gramophone. I came to associate sad wartime Bournemouth with it, but soon I was playing that music all too often in the London Philharmonic, its repetition making it for me just sentimental and boring, for it was Rachmaninov's Second Piano Concerto, so popular then because of its use in that sentimental film, *Brief Encounter*.

Malcolm Arnold joined the LPO as second trumpet early in 1941 and, soon after that, Geoffrey Gilbert, the first flute, was called up for military service and joined the Coldstream Guards band. The second flute moved up to be principal, leaving his place vacant, so Malcolm told the orchestral management about me and I was given a trial fortnight without audition.

"I'm going to the best orchestra in the world," I told everyone before resigning from the dreadful Bournemouth orchestra, bragging which didn't go down very well with my now ex-colleagues. I gave Reginald Goodall my bicycle as a gratefully accepted parting gift, and took the train to London.

LPO

The LPO was the orchestra I played with the longest, from 1941 to '50 and 1961 to '70 – eighteen years altogether; but it was touch and go whether I got started with them at all.

On the journey to Kingston-on-Thames for my first rehearsal I got to Waterloo station on time, but somehow missed the right train. Eventually getting there on a later one, I wandered about, first unable to find the theatre, and then unable to find the stage door. At last, small and alone, I went to the side of the stage and stood in the shadows alongside the brilliantly lit orchestra which was already rehearsing. Malcolm was among the brass raised up to the left, my only friend; to the right at my level, Sir Adrian Boult was conducting, tall, red-faced and ferociously moustached, his bald head shining under the theatrical lighting; and my empty chair was beyond the tightly-packed rows of busily bowing violins. Terrified of the brilliantly lit walk to it and of being stared at by so many alien faces, I panicked, decided to return to London and walked away – but, then with what seemed a heroic act of will, changed my mind and stumbled in, jostling bowing arms on the way.

Prokofiev's *Love For Three Oranges* was being rehearsed and, after quickly unpacking my instrument, the first thing I had to play was a rapid, exposed passage in unison with the first flute. Terrified and unnerved, I made a total hash of it, of course. Sir Adrian stopped the orchestra and made me fumble alone through the notes not just once but several times, and I was aware of the eighty professional musicians who listened, watched and waited for the incompetent newcomer. Eventually I got it right and the rehearsal continued. Between the rehearsal and concert, several players spoke to me in a kind and friendly way, cheering me up.

Adrian Boult (Photo Douglas Whittaker, principal flute, BBC Symphony Orchestra)

In the course of the next few weeks I quickly settled into the orchestral routine – and I passed my trial fortnight. But that first rehearsal was a foretaste of the total loss of face against which all orchestral musicians have to toughen themselves. Later on, taking into account my depressive tendency, I found it best to lower my self-esteem; then, knowing myself to be a fool, nobody could *make* a fool of me; thinking myself a second-rate musician, I wouldn't mind being told so. And, in compensation, there was the thought that my depression could soon be alleviated by having sex, any sex, quickly; and casual sex *did* make me feel better for a time. Mutual masturbation was easy to find in towns that had no street lighting and where young soldiers away from home needed it as much as I did.

In the orchestra, I came to have the same nonchalant attitude as the toughest of my new colleagues, many of whom I quickly got to know and like.

I very much liked Arthur, the first flute, who sat on my left. He was a typical orchestral musician of that time and, like so many, had learnt his trade of music in an army band. An orphan from a military family, he'd been educated (if that's the right word) at the Duke of York school in Kent, which was free for sons of soldiers killed in action. It may be a good school now, but then, by Arthur's account, it had brutal staff, inadequate food, and a military regime that reduced the boys to stunned servitude (good future soldiers, I suppose – and perhaps even good orchestral musicians). When a frightened little new boy arrived, he was trussed up in ropes by the others and put on a large chest in the middle of a stone floor; the older boys then threw pillows at him until he fell off. If the boy looked unpleasant when injured, the others locked him away for the night in a dark cupboard. This was a 'tradition of the school', so the staff didn't stop it. Arthur wouldn't hear a word spoken against the school, even when telling these stories; it had made a man of him, he said. I don't know what he meant by that, but, in spite of his upbringing, he was a friendly, pleasant man. Small and thin, with protruding teeth, he was proud of his sexual prowess, so proud that he would sometimes introduce himself to strangers by saying, "Ackroyd's me name; all prick and teeth". He said that he often had sex with lesbians, explaining that in their clubs there were usually one or two left over at the end of the evening who'd failed to find partners and were so desperate for sex that one of them would agree to go even with him. "Better than all that farting about with ordinary girls who won't fuck first time."

Jack, a foxy-looking man with a thin pencil-line moustache, the first oboe of the orchestra, was Arthur's closest friend, and they'd been at that school together. Both were happily married, and were also having it off with a couple of sexy young sisters. One day, Jack's wife came across a letter to Jack from one of the sisters which revealed what Jack and Arthur were up to. Jack, on being faced with this, managed to plead innocent and to put all the blame onto Arthur. She later rang Arthur's wife and told her all about Arthur's sins; and so Arthur had a bad time at home for some months and felt betrayed by his oldest friend. They had a huge row and then refused to speak to each other, even though they sat side by side in the orchestra every working day. So on musical matters they communicated angrily through me. For instance, during a rehearsal, Arthur turned right to me (Jack sat on his left) and growled, "Would you tell that fucking oboe player that he's fucking half a tone flat on that fucking D sharp." I then leant across Arthur and said to Jack, "There seems to be some difficulty over that D sharp; d'you think it'd be a good idea if you and Arthur tried tuning it together?"

Arthur gave me one heartfelt piece of advice: "Never, ever forget," he said, "that the conductor is your natural enemy."

Having been brought up first in that army school and then in the ranks of the army itself, people were for him divided into two sorts: the oppressed (his equals) and an inhuman boss class (school teachers, army-officers and conductors). Bullying conductors were accepted by him as natural, what he was used to, so he was comfortable playing for his enemies.

Arthur also said, "There's only two things in a musician's work; either you're bored to death or you're scared to death."

I thought about this and understood what he meant, and I heard it said many times by other players. But I decided that I was unusual, for I found delight and happiness as well. Just as a carpenter enjoys his skill and looks at his beautifully-made chair or cupboard with pleasure, so I hugely enjoyed, for instance, being perfectly in tune in a chord or playing a phrase exactly as I thought it should go. I more than enjoyed the thrilling sounds that were all around me and those which I made myself, and I also enjoyed mixing with the strange and at first incomprehensible people in the orchestra. They talked with emotion of pubs which had especially good draught Bass and told heartless jokes about 'juicy bits of E flat crumpet' (crumpet being slang for desirable women), who had 'old cows' as mothers. (the E flat trumpet is a tiny trumpet, so 'E flat *crumpet'* is very young girls). All very complicated and hard for me to learn. They said they hated music, and with them I would never have admitted that I enjoyed some of it, for that would have been seen as comical and I'd have been classed as an inferior amateur. First I learnt to play by their rules, then it all became quite easy and natural – playing it their way was then as easy as not picking my nose in public was with the people I'd been brought up with. New conventions learnt.

Surprisingly little resentment was expressed from the orchestra about my pacifism, perhaps because, being unfit or fake unfit themselves, some of them felt guilty about not fighting in the war themselves; but, all the same, I found it hard being in two unhappy minority groups, homosexual and pacifist. The general psychiatric opinion then was that homosexuality was caused by immaturity. Freud, very much believed in then, expressed the opinion that homosexuality was natural in adolescence, and that most people then moved on to heterosexuality, but that only homosexuals got stuck – but *could* become hetero with the right effort or with psychoanalysis. (How plain silly that idea seems now!) Then, when I met Sheila, a young woman I liked very much, and rather liked having sex with, I thought that I would grow up and thus become heterosexual just by being with her; and in addition she strongly supported my pacifism which helped me bear being in *that* minority group. We moved into a flat together in 1942 and two years later got married. We got on quite well, but I had some secret casual gay sex to keep me sane, easily done as I was spending so much time on orchestral tours all around the country.

After having sex with Sheila I used to have the weird sensation of being two people, of being split in half, and I can now guess what this meant. During sex it's normal not only to experience our own pleasure but also to imagine the pleasure we're giving to our partner. I was doing the latter so excessively that I was imagining being Sheila having sex with me, and suppressing my own feelings, thus avoiding heterosexual sex with her. *I* was the one being fucked. Getting out of bed afterwards, I was still in this fantasy and thus had the experience of being split in two.

Before living together we discussed my homosexuality, which seemed not to worry her much. She told me that she too had a psychological peculiarity, a horror of pregnancy, which upset her so much that she would become ill at the sight of a pregnant woman. I believed that our two peculiarities would balance out, not remembering the old saying that two negatives don't make a positive.

When I looked for somewhere for us to live together, it had to be Bloomsbury, partly for its recent literary associations but also because it was near railway stations, good for getting home to after provincial concerts. London was almost empty in the middle of the war, and asking in an estate agent's office if they had somewhere up to a maximum rent of two pounds a week, I was handed two fistfuls of keys with attached addresses and spent a happy afternoon looking at flats. The one I chose was on the top floor of an eighteenth-century house in Great Ormond Street. By great good luck I had come to London just a few days after the end of the intense bombing of the blitz, and having a skylight in our sitting room didn't worry us even during occasional air raids, but three years later the flying bombs were so disturbing there that (after we had tried and failed to sleep on the concrete floor in Holborn Underground station) we went each night to the basement of my aunt's solidly built house in St John's Wood.

At this later time the government, out of bravado, kept the Proms going while the flying bombs were falling. The orchestra sat playing under the Albert Hall's heavy acoustic stage canopy and I imagined a bomb coming crashing down through the hall's glass dome, breaking the canopy's slender supporting wires, the orchestra crushed to death by the canopy, the audience crushing itself to death in the panic.

After I had been second flute for a year (I'm going back to 1942 now), Arthur and Jack and some other wind players left to join the Liverpool Philharmonic, which for some reason I don't understand got exemption from the army for its players, whereas the London Phil. didn't. 'Gone with the Woodwind' was Johnny's joke then, for the film of almost that name had just arrived in England. Johnny, a Welsh viola player, was the orchestral clown, a genius at inventing jokes.

When Arthur left, I took over his job as first flute, and then stayed with the orchestra for eight more years; his leaving was another bit of luck, for I had by then almost enough knowhow for me to cope more or less, and by the end of the war I'd been made into a real professional.

During the war, we played popular programmes with all the British conductors of the time, and Sir Adrian Boult was one who travelled and worked with us often.

He was a handsome man, in spite of an over-large, fleshy nose, tall and healthy-looking, with a resonant, 1930s upper-class voice. He was friendly to us in a stand-offish way, never unkind or inconsiderate – though I must say that his getting me to play alone on my first rehearsal with the orchestra in Kingston was insensitive to say the least. Before the war he'd been disliked by the BBC Symphony Orchestra, partly because they found his music-making dull, but much more because, as their principal conductor, he had the responsibility for sacking and replacing players. All 'permanent' conductors are disliked for this reason, for changes have to be made and no player wants to see his colleagues hurt, or maybe fear to be the next to go. That's why visiting conductors are often liked better than resident ones. The LPO liked Boult but without admiration.

He did have a feeling for the shape of the music, liking long phrases and few climaxes. He knew where the loudest point of a symphony should be, and, in rehearsal made us giggle by shouting, "PUT THE LID ON IT," when the main climax arrived. But his sense of form didn't interest us, and we were irritated by his vague, floppy beat and lack of attention to detail. It was an orchestral joke that he'd had the cheek to write a book on conducting technique, and we felt we could get away with gross imprecision without his noticing, and did so when tired or lazy. For instance, before a concert with him in the Dome at Brighton, the horn players and I got drunk on Draught Bass in the bar in the theatre across the road from the hall; and then we staggered back to the Dome to play *Till Eulenspiegel*, which has a rapid flute part. I thought I played all right, and perhaps I did, but I wouldn't have got drunk before playing *Till* with most other conductors.

But, all the same, I was impressed when he conducted Elgar, and even more so during Schubert's Great C major Symphony. The Dream of Gerontius (pronounced with a *hard* G, he insisted) is the most revered music of Elgar, but for orchestras it's just plain boring. Boult was besotted with it and I saw him getting emotionally hotter as it played, restraining his tears with difficulty – while we longed for it to end. At what seems to be an emotional high-point in the first part of it, Gerontius himself slowly and sadly sings the words, "Use well the interval"; the players then lift their right arms and mime drinking glasses of beer. (Those words are as meaningless to me now as then, for I've no idea what Gerontius is all about, even after playing it hundreds of times.)

Except when conducting a few especially loved pieces, Boult usually seemed to be a mild and detached person; but now and then, for what seemed to be a trivial reason, he would suddenly lose his cool, go purple in the face, and storm about, shouting and stamping. We'd try to laugh it off, but really felt a bit alarmed.

Once, rehearsing Ravel's *Daphnis*, he conducted the flute solo so slowly that it was almost impossible to play, so in the rehearsal interval I politely asked him if he could possibly speed it up a bit. It's against all propriety for a player to suggest tempos to a conductor, and Boult wasn't pleased. In the concert he unkindly got it going so absurdly fast that again it was almost unplayable.

He took considerable trouble learning the surnames of all the players but didn't give the impression of actually *liking* them (and it was always 'Sir Adrian' and 'Mr. Adeney' between us, even after thirty years). He was closest to Wally Knight, the cockney chap who handled the baggage, harps and double basses; that straightforward servant-master relationship he could cope with, for it was simpler than the ones with the orchestra.

Either Wally or the orchestra's leader would often be asked nervously by him before going onto the platform for a concert, "Check that my flies are done up all right," as though he couldn't do this himself. Compare this with Klemperer. A few years later, on the platform at the start of a concert in the Festival Hall, Hugh Bean, the leader of the Philharmonia, said sotto voce, "Doctor Klemperer, your fly-buttons are undone"; and Klemperer muttered gruffly back, "And vot has zat to do viz Beethoven?"

Just as I'd found Arthur's army-private personality hard to understand at first, so it was with Boult's army-officer type, but worrying about such things was far from my mind at that time of extreme overwork. Before joining the LPO I'd wafted along with maximum freedom and minimum responsibility, and then was suddenly plunged into a work and travel routine which was so exhausting that rest and sleep were the greatest longed-for luxuries. We sometimes played fourteen concerts in a week; for instance, we once had two concerts a day from Monday to Friday in Edinburgh, then an all-night train journey to London, a Saturday afternoon concert at Luton and back for an evening concert at the Albert Hall in London. I knew almost none of the music and spent my precious spare time learning any quick solo bits, but leaving the tuttis to luck, desperately trying not to make a total fool of myself. Before concerts, I'd find a place to be alone (often a loo cubicle) and concentrate on what was coming, quietly gaining energy for playing, thinking of the wartime audience waiting for us, needing the music. Knowing the value of music for those audiences, that they were listening to it like starving people at a meal, helped some of us to get through our endless work schedule.

This wartime musical life was a mixture of fatigue, excitement and boredom. The all-night train journeys were a dreary nightmare, and often very cold, for, to save energy, all train heating was turned off, and they were almost dark, for train lights were dimmed so that they couldn't be seen from German bombers. Jolting along in a third-class seat and failing to sleep, I found you could go through to the end of extreme fatigue and come out for a time to a brightness of new energy – but then you paid for it later by feeling even worse. To pass the time, I played solo whist for money with Arthur, amongst others, and lost heavily at first. Arthur just laughed; but he later relented and taught me how to play the game properly, and I won some of the money back. Keeping to my middle-class ways, I also played chess and read the whole of Proust, sleepless under the thin shaft of shrouded train light. A tall, shabby old violinist called George taught me chess and, although it became my ambition, I never got near to beating him.

Sometimes food was scarce on tour, but this didn't worry me, for the young can miss meals less unhappily than the old, and I watched with contempt when a fat old violinist was so hungry that he went into a field, pulled up a turnip and gnawed at it.

Fatigue, hunger and sexual stress can have strange effects, especially if all occur at the same time. One cold winter evening in Cardiff I returned to my dreary hotel room in the deepest depressed exhaustion, having been travelling and playing endlessly for days on end, having eaten almost nothing that day and recently having had no sex of the kind I wanted. I fell onto the bed with a moan and turned out the light. There was at once an astonishing feeling of a calming presence in the room, for it seemed that a human-sized being was standing near the end of the bed. I stared into the darkness with unnaturally wide-open eyes. My heart beat fast. Having been inward-turning and self-pitying, my attention turned outward and away from myself, and I listened to sounds from the street; I heard Big Ben chiming on the radio downstairs and people talking in the corridor outside, all at the same time as sensing this presence. Then the presence and the feeling of powerful benevolence gradually lessened.

Later, I thought I'd had a mystical experience, but now see it as like those often reported near-death levitations, white lights, dark tunnels and heaven which are caused by the malfunctioning of the dying brain. Hunger and stress, like dying, disrupt the brain.

I don't know how this fairly common sort of experience affects others, but it turned me from being a self-regarding adolescent into someone just a bit more adult, for afterwards I was more aware of other people's feelings, and became much more relaxed in relating to them.

At about this time Sheila and I went to a concert in London's Conway Hall. During the concert I noticed that on the arch over the stage was written part of Polonius's advice to Hamlet: 'To thine own self be true'.

I puzzled over this. To *which* of my selves should I be true? Did I even *have* a self?

Jokes and Conductors

In London in 1941, I did my first recording, which was background music for a John Gielgud production of *Macbeth*. The sessions were at Abbey Road studios. Nowadays, the Musicians' Union usually won't allow recorded music for the stage ('Keep music live'), but during the war they were less fussy.

I'd never played to a microphone before and was scared, heart thumping every time it was in use. Since then I've spent thousands of hours in Abbey Road, terrifying hours, boring hours, exciting hours, but none more exciting than those first sessions of William Walton's music for *Macbeth*. Gielgud himself was there, and his presence made it all the more important – and after the sessions he followed me on to a bus (surely such a famous actor wouldn't usually take a bus), which made a good end to my day; but, as he was so old, I moved from the seat where I was being stared at and went upstairs. I've worked out recently that he was then thirty-seven. For the very young, almost everyone is old, and the conductors also then all seemed ancient.

Sir Henry Wood, though, really was old, for I knew him only at the end of his career. I had what seemed then a triumph playing the scherzo from Mendelssohn's *Midsummer Night's Dream* in London with him. It was new to me and I didn't know of its then supposed great difficulty for the flute. Any present-day amateur flute-player could manage it now, but I recently heard a pre-war recording of it by Toscanini with the BBC orchestra in which it is completely fucked up. Very odd.

The concert was unrehearsed, but I had time to practise the part beforehand and found I could manage the whole semi-quaver bit at the end in one breath. Playing it well in the performance, the very end was spoilt by the second flute, an old and experienced player, who was so worried for me that he lost concentration and miscounted his bars, causing cacophony. Afterwards I was overwhelmed by praise from the orchestra and from Sir Henry, and at that time I desperately needed support.

I gradually came to feel that the other players in the LPO liked my playing and liked me; I liked them too and enjoyed the knowledge of their back-up when I was playing and the warm comfort of being part of a community.

Sir Henry was a funny old cove when I knew him, not at all the unpleasant, rude man he was said to have been when young. For instance, he'd told a solo cellist whose playing annoyed him, "Madam, you have that *magnificent* instrument between your legs, and all you can do is *scratch* it."

And when he was young he was considered odd and eccentric. An old violinist told me, for instance, that, after a concert, Wood had gone to the gents' lavatories at the Albert Hall and said to the young attendant, "I'm feeling rather tired. Please will you undo my fly-buttons and take out my cock for me?" Surely, it seems to me now, this was a request for sexual relief after an exciting concert; but it was told to me with no sexual implication, just as an illustration of his eccentricity.

Before the First World War he brought to England good orchestral players from the continent who had shown the ignorant English how to play. This made him very unpopular with the musicians who were displaced, or whose livelihoods were threatened, but it laid the foundations for the superb present-day English orchestral playing.

He was a small, fat man with short legs – a waddler. He used a huge baton that sometimes swung with a rhythm of its own, to be ignored. He wore an absurd old, shabby tail suit. During a Promenade Concert in the Albert Hall his braces broke and the trousers slowly fell, exposing more and more of awful, old, off-white long-johns. Delighted, the orchestra watched as they played, but when the trousers had got almost to his knees he gave a mighty hitch-up, and managed to hang onto them with one hand to the end of the piece, through applause and the walk off the stage.

In the Albert Hall, with Wood conducting, there was for me the hugely exciting event of my first solo appearance – the flute obbligato to 'Lo, Hear the Gentle Lark'. The soprano, even prouder than Nellie Melba of her Australian origin, called herself Austra Bourne. She looked like a film star and for the performance she wore a superb white gown with a long train. Coming on to play, I nervously followed close behind her and, half way across the large platform, there was the sound of ripping silk. She stopped and I bumped into her.

"*Get off my train*", she hissed.

In his old age Wood rehearsed by rote. At one point in the Eroica, for instance, he would always say mournfully to the 'cellos, "Sorrow-laden crotchets." During the interval of the rehearsal, I looked at his score and saw pencilled at the right place the very words, 'sorrow-laden crotchets'. Later on in the score, at a place not yet reached in rehearsal, I found the words, 'violins sharp'. Duly, when we came to play that passage, he said in his squeaky, Cockney, complaining voice, "Violins, you're sharp."

He rewrote the classics, so that everything sounded comfortably late nineteenth century; for instance he completely changed the scoring of Beethoven's First Symphony, making it as rich-sounding as Brahms. He cut out chunks of symphonies for fear of boring audiences; in Tchaikovsky's Fifth, alternate groups of two bars disappeared (play two, cut two) for a large part of the first movement, and he also made big cuts in the other movements. The orchestra heartily approved. For players, there was 'good' and 'bad' music, so Beethoven's Fifth was good because it lasts for only about thirty-five minutes, but his Ninth was very bad at seventy. Schubert's Fifth was excellent. Brahms's First was worse than his Third. Beethoven's Violin Concerto much worse than Mendelssohn's. A good concert was one that lasted for less than two hours.

Johnny Cload, an amiable Welsh viola player, was the great expert. "How long is Brahms One?" I asked him just before playing it.

"Well, with a *good* conductor it lasts forty-three minutes, but with 'Timber' (meaning Wood) now he's so old it might be as bad as forty-seven".

Johnny, with his sad-clown's face, as well as being a timer of music, was a great inventor of nicknames. Once he had named a flimsy-looking little violinist 'the kipper', you just saw a kipper and never again the violinist. His description of Basil Cameron's high-arm conducting as 'a man struggling to get his head out of a sack' was so accurate that I could never again take Cameron seriously. Sargent was 'the Chinese General', and a very small double-bass player, who disappeared under his instrument when carrying it, was called 'the moth', but 'Timber' for Wood was invented before Johnny's day. Johnny had the strange habit of suddenly proclaiming in a loud theatrical voice, and in any context, "Oh, the *agony* of it." What the agony was, I never found out.

As well as with Wood and Boult, I also played a lot with Sargent, my *bête noire*, and he'll be a running joke in this book. He was satisfied when we played the right notes, but he seemed to have little feeling for music and much for his public image. He looked good: slim and strong-armed with a brown, thin, handsome face and black, smooth hair. He moved like a dancer, but his movements gave information to the audience rather than to the orchestra. Fearful of losing control, he had the irritating habit of dividing slow, flowing music into little flicking beats; for instance, he conducted the opening solo flute of 'L'Après-midi d'un faune' in quaver jabs – most off-putting for the player. I put up with this, but, later on, Gareth Morris, principal flute of the Philharmonia, boldly asked him in rehearsal if he would please conduct the passage more smoothly, rather than in little jerks. Sargent was furious, and Gareth was ordered off the platform to see him and Walter Legge, the boss of the orchestra in Legge's office. Then Gareth had a surprise, for Sargent declared that he absolutely refused to conduct an orchestra in which he was referred to as a little jerk.

Sargent battled with orchestras, seeming to think that he would be humiliated if ever caught off guard. Perhaps he was just plain frightened of us. So in this self-created battle he took any opportunity to humili-ate a player who made a slip or who found something difficult to play, by emphasising this to the rest of the orchestra, and perhaps even forc-ing some unhappy young back-desk violinist to make a public fool of himself in rehearsal by telling him to play alone a passage that he hadn't seen before and which was plainly beyond his abilities.

Amazingly bad at getting on with his players, he put backs up wherever he worked, yet was loved and admired by amateur singers and had an excellent relationship with the renowned Huddersfield Choral Society. He was sometimes helpful and generous to people in trouble and I have seen him weep when conducting Elgar, so perhaps he was more complicated than I then thought. He was one of many conductors we found boring and objectionable, and he was one of the many who talked too much. We didn't mind being told that we were too loud or too soft, too fast or too slow (though too sharp or too flat is getting a bit personal), but we objected strongly to waffle about the inner meaning of the music. I soon learnt not to hear when a conductor talked about the music, and got some rest and time to think about other things, perhaps silently practising a difficult passage, covertly solving a crossword puzzle, or just thinking about what I'd eat for lunch. My mind was set to hear the conductor say, "start again from letter B" or whatever, or the word "flute", which meant that he was talking to me, and not to hear anything else. There must be literally thousands of hours of conductors' talk that I simply haven't heard a word of.

Recently, a player ran a stop-watch each time a certain conductor stopped the rehearsal and talked. The talking time added up to an hour and forty minutes of a three-hour rehearsal – which is plenty of pleasant dreaming time for the orchestra. Indifference to and contempt of conductors is a necessary part of an orchestral player's armour. How else could he stand the humiliation of these megalomaniacs ranting and raving at him? How else survive the boredom of hearing conductors' views on music?

Although I was serious about playing the flute, most of what went on in the orchestra was ludicrous. Or perhaps I remember only the ludicrous things, and I remember them in small scenes. For instance, Sargent's expression when Malcolm Arnold mimicked another player's voice saying "silly fucker" just behind Sargent's back; EJ Moeran, the composer, coming on to the Albert Hall platform to bow to applause for his new work, but so drunk that he couldn't straighten up again and

While the conductor speaks (Photo RA)

meandering off with his face at knee level; a cor anglais player trying to play his solo in the Flying Dutchman Overture, not realising that its cleaning mop was stuck up its bell, causing squeaks, not notes; myself making a ludicrous hash of a simple flute solo in 'La Mer', followed by audible giggles from around me; being intolerably bored in rehearsal – when *will* this ever end? – being pompously ticked off by Sargent for making a small slip in rehearsal; the frustrated anger of wanting to get back at him.

But now I'll try to re-experience the malice of the angry youth I was then by relating a nasty incident. In London during the war, Sargent was sharing a taxi with the LPO's manager, Tom Russell. Sirens wailed like vast, mad sopranos and bombs fell near by. The usually perfectly-behaved Sargent, with a perfect red carnation in his perfect suit, was terrified. He wailed, he wept, then he rolled into a foetal position on the floor of the taxi, sucking his thumb. Tom disliked Sargent, so next day he told the orchestra what had happened, with glee and pretended embarrassment.

There were other, pleasanter conductors. Cameron (the one who conducted as though struggling to get out of a sack) had a long and successful career and, although he seemed to be typically English, I was told that he had changed his name from von Hindenburg during the First World War. I've since discovered that the truth was more complicated: he was born Cameron, but in 1912 changed his name to von Hindenburg because British conductors were not then taken seriously. In 1914 he had to revert quickly to Cameron or be in bad trouble. (Stokowski to Stokes and back to Stokowski also happened around that time.) I played innumerable concerts with him, but can't remember a single one, though I do remember him, although fussy, as relaxing and not frightening to play for. He lived alone, was a very hard worker and never took holidays, he had no interest except music and was depressed with leisure. When old and conducting in the Albert Hall, he had a non-fatal stroke; the St John's Ambulance people carried him off the stage, unconscious, on a stretcher, but still clutching his baton – and still beating four beats to the bar.

George, the kind old violinist who had taught me to play chess, said that Cameron, like Wood, had been rude and aggressive to players when young, but had, like so many, become benign only with age.

George was famous in the orchestra for an ancient, drink-stained tail-suit, even worse than Wood's, and for his enormous dirty, black boots which he wore all day as well as for concerts. Johnny said he even slept in them. Like most of the orchestra, he drank huge quantities of beer and one evening before a concert he overdid it. During a long symphony, he peed into his old trousers and down his legs, and after that he was always known as Piss-In, for Johnny had named him 'Piss in Boots'.

Because of George's tuition, I was able to play chess with a viola player called Wrayburn Glasspool, a remarkable man, and with him chess

Wrayburn Glasspool at Glyndebourne (Photo RA)

somehow became a jokey, jovial game. I took a lot of trouble to learn the conventional opening moves, but Ray would sometimes make my knowledge redundant by playing some absurd opening move such as pawn to rook three, which would nullify all my knowledge of conventional opening moves, and then beat me. He first played viola with the LPO in 1935, and continued playing in the orchestra for nearly sixty years. A record? Guinness? During the whole of that time he had been covertly writing music and, except for a very pleasant flute sonata which he wrote for me during the war, I have heard none of it. What is hidden in his cupboards at home? He is highly intelligent, so I think it must be interesting.

I liked Ray very much, enjoyed our jovial relationship and admired his wiry physique and rather swarthy good looks. I would have loved to have had sex with him, but of course made no move in that direction, knowing I'd be rebuffed and our friendship ended, but the warmth of my feeling for him made my marriage more manageable, diluting the heterosexuality.

Sheila liked Ray and also got on well with others in the orchestra, especially Charles and Boris, two proselytising Communists. They lent me a book by Engels which I found unbearably dull and only pretended to read to the end. Because of my ignorance, stupidity and lack of interest, they invariably won our political arguments; but I'd read Arthur Koestler on Stalin's recent political trials, giving me a very different point of view about what went on in Russia. So, even when they insisted that Koestler was merely a 'capitalist lackey' and so I should ignore his writing, I still stayed doubtful about Communism. But our political arguments were neither frequent nor heated, so we spent much happy time together, going to the best provincial restaurants, where we gossiped and laughed as we ate delicious meals of off-the-ration Spam and chips, swilled down with lots of draught Bass.

Boris was a brilliant 'cellist, but had no solo career because of a shake of his bowing arm when nervous, causing a tremolo on long notes known as the 'pearlies', for the bow then bumps along the strings as though strung with pearls instead of horse-hair; it happens especially to back-desk players who suddenly have to play by themselves. In Rossini's *William Tell Overture*, for instance, there are two slow solo notes for one of the back-desk 'cellos; the wind players, who are used to playing alone, hear the pearlies with superior and malicious pleasure.

Boris was a handsome man, especially seen in profile from the audience. During the war there were no pop-stars for young girls to adore, so Boris was put into this role and was mobbed after concerts and was sent bottles of almost unobtainable whisky by a rich woman. He disliked this stardom, but I, as the second-best-looking player in the orchestra, only pretended to dislike my slightly lower level of attention, but really enjoyed the crowds of autograph-hunters at stage doors, the adulation and the love letters, the offers of marriage and even an offer to darn my socks.

Sheila saw through my pretence and mocked my vanity. She also mocked my flute-playing, saying, after she had been to a concert and heard me playing emotionally, "Oh, you and your randy-shepherd-boy flute style." It had been in Brahms's Fourth Symphony, which always got me into a fever of emotion whenever I played it. (Throughout my career I played all music in a style only suitable for Debussy, with lots of vibrato, and I now see that Sheila was right to object to my playing of Brahms. What a pity I didn't see it then.) She probably also saw that I was putting into playing the emotion and sexuality I gave only more weakly to her.

I didn't much mind her teasing and we got along amiably most of the time. It now seems absurd that, in the middle of a desperate war, I should get fussed about playing a wrong note or get such huge delight from playing well; Sheila saw it as absurd and I didn't.

She was an excellent and inventive cook, and even during the worst wartime food shortages, we ate well. At the start of the war she taught history, but then later on did boring and tiring ambulance work. She disliked wearing the ugly, unbecoming uniform, for she was good looking and naturally enjoyed admiration, and when she was in civilian clothes I liked being seen with her, thinking us a pretty pair; but privately her large breasts, narrow waist and wide hips were for me repulsive to look at, though surprisingly pleasant to feel in bed when the light was out, and we had what I suppose was a standard sex-life.

In 1945, as well as a general election (the one in which Attlee replaced Churchill) there were local council elections. The local Labour Party agent asked Sheila to stand for election on to Holborn Borough Council (now part of Camden).

"You do realise, don't you," he said to her, "that Holborn is true-blue Tory, almost entirely a business area; so we'll have a good time, do a bit of canvassing, have some parties and get defeated."

Sheila agreed to stand and then found that the agent had obtained almost only pretty young women as his team. She and the others put in a lot of work, did have a good time, and, much to their surprise, were all elected. Result, the most glamorous borough council ever known.

Apart from the orchestra and our families, our friends were mostly from Sheila's recent Oxford days, where she'd been a student at Somerville. Peter, now Sir Peter, Strawson used to turn up in his army uniform, and Ann, his future wife, was for a time a third sharer in our flat. Later on Peter became an eminent philosopher and settled in Oxford. In a quiet and gentle way he was highly critical and intelligent, and during the last fifty years or so I'd been in the habit of putting fantasy philosophical questions to him. "What do you say, Peter, to this problem?" and go off into a dreamy talk with him, and get a fantasy chiding for my silliness. I would occasionally meet the real Peter and feel very shy, and then, to my present blushing-in-bed sort of embarrassment, once sent him a bit of philosophy on the subject of perception that I'd written. He wrote back kindly, and even talked to me about it when I visited him and Ann in Oxford, but I was too ill-at-ease and distracted to understand what he was on about, except that obviously he thought I'd written nonsense. Anyway, my fantasy relationship with him makes a real one too difficult, for I assume that my fantasy-Peter and the real one have evolved separately into two totally different people.

It may well be that my present philosophical thoughts are as crackpot as my theory at the start of this book that babies get themselves born because they're bored in the womb, and someone will turn up who'll prove it to me; but it hasn't happened yet and I still spend time thinking about them. I did a year's philosophy at Birkbeck College in order to find out more, but it didn't help, and my tutor there, to whom I once spoke about my ideas, was scornful of them. Several of my friends, as well as Peter, have read what I have to say and none thought it made sense, so I tend to see myself as a silly old man with a bee in his bonnet.

I sent this chapter, more or less as it stands now, to Peter and Ann in Oxford, explaining that I was expanding the memoir of my musical experiences I'd already shown them and making it more personal – meaning that I'd include references to marriage and homosexuality.

Peter replied affectionately, and as part of his letter he wrote: "Ann and I found your original memoir extremely entertaining as it stood; and though I have no doubt it could profitably be expanded, I would hesitate to make it more 'personal': the result might simply be embarrassing, which, of all things, we English like to avoid."

On reading this, I hear Peter's jokey, ironical voice saying, "We English," and tend to agree with him; but then I think, "Are we really so easily embarrassed nowadays? Surely we've now become less easily upset by personal openness than we used to be." We carry old values along with new ones, so I may feel embarrassment on publication, but didn't I choose to be a public performer, an exhibitionist? Yes, of course I did; so I may as well go on being one, and I might even enjoy a tingle of excitement. I've been a virtuoso chameleon for too long, forever timidly changing my behaviour to fit in with the people around me; so now I'm trying in this book to describe what I'm really like – though I expect that some other people, as well as Peter if he were still alive, for he died in 2006, would dislike my frankness.

Knowing Peter and Ann for so long has made me go forward more than fifty years, and now I'll return to earlier times.

Beecham

Sir Thomas Beecham founded the LPO in 1932 and it flourished. But in September 1939 entertainment in Britain was forbidden, for the government, fearful of immediate German bombing, closed all concert halls, cinemas and theatres – though it very soon changed its mind about this. Beecham was abroad and the LPO went bankrupt.

The players, dominated by a dynamic little viola player called Tom Russell, formed a committee, got financial backing, and set about bringing much-needed music to wartime audiences.

In 1944 Beecham came back to England from the United States, a perilous crossing with a risk of sinking by U-boat. He conducted many concerts with his old orchestra, even though he knew that the orchestra was then being run by an elected committee, and he didn't any longer have complete control of finance, personnel and programmes. And, until the inevitable conflict between democracy and dictatorship came, there were memorable concerts.

The first was after a short orchestral holiday, so we were not as exhausted as usual. I'd never played with a great conductor before, and the players had talked a lot about him, so I had a worrying picture of a wonderful but overpowering father; and I knew some of his records well, and was impressed by them.

Arthur had said, during a rehearsal with Boult, "When Tommy comes back we won't be able to get away with playing as scruffy as this any more."

Beecham was a frightening myth; and Johnny had no nickname for him, which was ominous.

Seeing him for the first time, I was surprised to see a small, fat man of much the same size and shape as Henry Wood; quite unlike his impressive photographs. Short legs. Another waddler. Although he looked so ordinary, his slow, pompous drawl was intimidating.

His first rehearsal started with Mendelssohn's *Midsummer Night's Dream Overture*, which begins with a series of very quiet wind chords, the first one for two flutes only. Scared stiff, and faced with an extraordinarily vague beat, I simply couldn't play. When did a chord start? I was foxed, but after many tries and much anxiety, I managed to make some sort of a go of playing and the chords continued, but raggedly and appallingly out of tune. (I hadn't then learnt how to cope with the many conductors who can't clearly indicate the start of wind chords. It is the first flute's job to guess what the conductor thinks he's up to, and then to lead the wind with a movement of his instrument. The chord will sound much later than the beat, but I've never known any conductor object to that.)

I thought Beecham was inconsiderate to expect his players to play well with so little technical help from him, but I didn't say so to my colleagues at the time, for he was their hero. My early judgement was right to see him as inconsiderate and selfish, but wrong to think that his vague beat would actually kill the music.

All orchestral musicians loved Sir Thomas, none Sir Malcolm Sargent. This was partly because of the different degree of their musical gifts and because one had a pleasant way of dealing with orchestras and the other didn't, but also for the following reason. In Britain, until after 1945, there was no public funding of music: no Arts Council, no grants to orchestras, and very little private funding either. There was Glyndebourne (funded by the Christies), a few orchestras – and Beecham. Beecham had been rich, for his family had made an all-purpose get-you-well pill containing mainly an antacid and rhubarb ('Beecham's pills, worth a guinea a Box') which had made them millionaires. Sir Thomas couldn't get his hands on the capital, but used the income from it and a great deal of begged and borrowed money in promoting music, first with his opera company, then with the LPO. In the 1930s there was severe unemployment among musicians, for cinemas had stopped using them to accompany silent films, the 'talkies' having arrived, so players were grateful to Beecham for employment at a time when they were often in danger of hunger. Sargent, as I was told many times, had said to a newspaper that "musicians play best on empty stomachs", a remark which they deeply resented, and some never forgave. Beecham filled those stomachs.

Actually, 'empty stomachs' was an exaggeration that had grown over the years. All that Sargent had really said (to the *Daily Telegraph*) was a much milder, "As soon as a man thinks he is in his orchestral job for life, with a pension waiting for him at the end of it, he tends to lose something of his supreme fire."

I knew Beecham only after his money had run out, when he had to work hard to get funding, and it seemed then that he was a great rogue, but a rogue one could identify with. After all, who wouldn't like to have the cheek to go to a very grand hotel, emphasising that you are Sir Thomas Beecham, Bart, get the best room, order champagne and expensive meals, complain about the appalling quality of the hotel and its service, and then leave without paying the bill? Who wouldn't like to make insulting speeches to audiences and get roars of applause in response. For instance, during a concert in Leicester, he said, as I remember it, in his slow, upper-crust drawl, his head held back disdainfully, "As is well known, the people of Leicester are totally without culture. This is the heartland of the Philistines. I am told that you make excellent pies, but here is a town with no art. It is extraordinary that we bring this great orchestra to this dreary town and its appalling people;" and they loved him for it, everyone snobbishly believing that he was criticising their neighbours, not themselves. (A few years earlier he had tried humour of this sort on the Australians who, being less self-assured than the people of Leicester, threw him, fully clothed, into a swimming-pool.)

And who wouldn't like to have had the cheek to hijack a charitable trust (the *Delius Society*) and use its considerable funds? With this money he financed for a time himself and his orchestra. Many years later, in 1983, I sat next to Eric Fenby, Delius's biographer and helper, on a long bus journey with the LSO across Florida, and I asked him about the *Delius Society*. He spoke angrily of Beecham's forceful taking over of the late Frederick Delius's money by making a trust and then getting control of this trust for his own use. Fenby was so angry and so voluble that I was glad when at last the bus got to Miami Airport.

In the 1940s I played in the LPO for *Delius Society* gramophone recordings at the Abbey Road studios. For each session Beecham turned up an hour late and worked for about ten minutes; then he would send us all home, delighted at being fully paid for a three-hour session. Beecham got paid too, of course, and there would be plenty of Delius's music left for future recordings.

But there was one who got the better of Beecham, the oboist Leon Goossens. I had, of course, listened to Beecham's pre-war records on which Leon would shine out so beautifully and so prominently. But he wasn't really a loud player. A few years later, when I was in the LPO myself (though Leon had left it by then), I was told by my colleagues who had been in the orchestra with him that he'd said, when recording orchestral music, "That as the oboe has many overtones which don't record well and make the instrument sound too quiet", he must sit alone, out in front of the rest of the woodwind. Thus he would be nearer the single microphone that was used in those days of mono recordings and would make symphonies sound like oboe concertos. As he played so very much better than any other oboist in London, and as Beecham feared losing him, this had to be agreed to.

But Goossens wasn't always so bossy. In the 1930s practically every musical person in Britain owned his recording of Mozart's oboe quartet. It was *the* top seller. Sadly, he hadn't been very clever money-wise, for he got no royalties from it and had been paid in total only three guineas. Well done the gramophone company!

I played this record hundreds of times during my early teens, overwhelmed by its beauty, and then learning from it and taking the style of playing to heart. He formed the style of mid-twentieth-century British wind playing, because almost every woodwind player of the time copied him. I wonder if *he* got *his* style from the cellist Casals; their playing had similarities. Both played with lavish vibrato and both had the same rubato styles – for instance, getting louder as they played rising passages, lingering for a rest on top notes and then scuttling down the other side. When they emphasised notes, both players lengthened them by playing them a tiny bit early (the opposite of those pianists who use awful, pregnant-pause delays for emphasis). This early playing of important notes causes an unpleasant shortening of upbeats, sounding very odd and unstylish now. Now, good players are more subtle.

The few wind players who resisted the Goossens influence, and who to my ears seemed stiff and wooden at the time, now sound on their old recordings beautifully stylish and twenty-first century. I'm thinking especially of the flute-player Gareth Morris and the clarinettist Bernard Walton. Nowadays Goossens's wide, slow vibrato, and the tricksy rubato, used regardless of what sort of music he played, sound archaic, even comical, so you need to take a historical leap to be able to enjoy what is still to be relished as heartfelt and virtuoso playing. And when I hear old recordings of my own playing, I dislike the vibrato I used, even though it was accepted then.

It wasn't until the 1960s that I first played with Goossens, a great day for me. He arrived early for the rehearsal and sat practising his music, not the late-arriving prima donna I'd expected. When I sat down next to him he was friendly, even jovial, and I was soon at ease. During the rehearsal there were many passages for flute and oboe in unison or in octaves, and afterwards he praised me for my intuitive ability to play with others. It wasn't intuition. Because of my study of his playing I knew *exactly* how he would shape every phrase, and even slowed down my vibrato so that we throbbed together.

Years later, when working with him, as I often did, I found him to be a most pleasant and likeable man, and for a short time we had a trio together, with Ivor Newton the pianist. Although he was the prima donna of the LPO, he was loyal to Beecham for many years, presumably because he appreciated Beecham's special musical qualities.

Beecham was full of warmth and love for music and was totally involved in getting the underfed, cynical, war-weary orchestra to feel as he did. He succeeded. Those ex-army toughs whose only interest in music had been how long a piece lasted and how soon they could get to the pub, now said how much they loved Berlioz and Mozart and actually admitted that they enjoyed the concerts. They really meant it and I agreed with them, for we were spell-bound, just as audiences were, by his ability to make music vivid.

He wasn't much concerned with the technical details of the orchestra, but left those to the players; he was very much concerned with the phrasing of tunes – where there should be emphases and where *diminuendos,* where there should be a warm sound and where a cooling off. He'd take a long time over a simple 'cello tune, but not mind if the accompaniment didn't quite fit with it. He rehearsed by gesture and singing, not trying to explain much verbally; so, unlike so many conductors, Beecham wasn't handicapped by lack of words in concerts.

In rehearsal, he would sing, shout, stamp, frown, scowl; and then suddenly relax and tell a silly story. He wasn't polite or flattering, he told mostly banal jokes (though a few good ones) and he didn't bother to learn his scores thoroughly, for I noticed that he knew only the tunes and not the other parts. When there was not simple two or three time, he nearly always got lost and caused chaos; even the more complicated bits of Sibelius and the five-beats-to-the-bar part of 'Daphnis and Chloe' foxed him, and one would have expected the players to have said, "This man's a rich charlatan," and stayed bored and minute-counting; but no, the whole orchestra woke up and put every bit of their energy into playing for him.

He talked to audiences and made them laugh and it seemed at the time that he was telling wonderful jokes. But afterwards I would think over what he'd said and, except when insulting people, he'd said nothing. No jokes. Nothing. Many sayings were wrongly attributed to him, even Sir Henry's abuse to the scratching 'cellist, but such blunt rudeness wasn't his style.

He was at his best with short, sensual music, especially in overtures and incidental music by Berlioz, Sibelius, Delius and Mozart. He made great music out of trashy nineteenth-century overtures, but he seemed less interested in the longer spans of Beethoven and Brahms symphonies. Today, some of his Mozart records sound stilted and unstylish, with every phrase sentimentally swelling and dying away, but, when playing in a live performance, his music was warm and caressing and I was totally involved and in agreement.

But it infuriated me that he'd usually turn up an hour or more late for rehearsal, without apology, keeping the tired orchestra hanging about when they so much needed that hour for extra sleep; but you couldn't count on his lateness and arrive late yourself. Some years earlier, a violinist called Ball (famous for Beecham asking him, "What is your name? Ball? How singular") arrived late for rehearsal, and for once Beecham was on time. Ball was sacked. But that was before the war, when the LPO was a tyranny, not yet a democracy.

In November 1945 the LPO played in Paris and Brussels with Beecham and Charles Munch (or 'Charlie Chew', as Johnny called him). The players had told me about previous foreign tours, but I'd learnt only of the orchestra's extreme drunkenness, nothing about the countries visited. Some players are scared of leaving England, so they get drunk at the port or airport when leaving England, and manage to stay drunk, opting out. But for me, leaving England for the first time after the war was just hugely exciting.

We travelled to France by train and boat, of course, and I was badly seasick when crossing the Channel, and still felt ill on the way from Calais to Paris. But, slowly recovering, I stared out of the window of the train at the strange little rectangular fields, the thin, red, detached houses, the great vista of flat landscape, and eventually in the evening the train steamed very slowly into Paris. I looked down at the suburbs and then at the city itself, more brightly lit than dismal post-war London. I'd seen only British cities before, so the streets crowded with oddly dressed people, the strange makes of cars, the cafés and bustling markets showed vividly that I'd got to another civilisation, something as alien to me then as a remote village in Bhutan would be now, and I looked forward to being in amongst this strangeness and to understanding it.

Paris was crowded with army personnel, so no hotel had been found for us. Instead, we were given a train of Wagons-Lits standing at a platform of the Gare de l'Est. Arriving there, being young and agile, I ran ahead and got myself one of the few first-class single compartments, with a comfortable bed and a little red bedside light – very cosy. We had to use the filthy station loos and eat in the station buffet, which had appalling food; the bread looked like bread but tasted like sawdust, coffee was burnt barley and we had no idea what the tough, stringy sausages were made of. Food was even scarcer in Paris than in London. We were used to rationing, even of potatoes and bread, but in Britain (I don't know why) coffee was unrationed and always plentiful. Bringing some to Paris, where it hadn't been tasted for years, was a good idea, and giving it to the people I met produced amazed gratitude.

I walked the Paris streets for hours, staring at the old, blue buses, the shabby houses, the smartly dressed, underfed crowds, and listened to new street sounds – bits of accordion music from cafés, drunk men singing strange songs, countrymen on squeaking old bicycles bringing in produce on little trailers, one even with a squealing pig. I visited Versailles by train, and then, back in Paris, went on the slow and strange-smelling Métro; but the greatest pleasure was the new freedom of being abroad after the long years of wartime England.

I picked up a young man, and, as I was to confirm often later on, I found that a sexual relationship with a resident is the quickest way to feel really part of a new place, no longer an outsider.

The orchestra played in the Théâtre des Champs Elysées, where we gave a good performance of Mozart's Jupiter Symphony, and a disgracefully bad one of Britten's Sea Interludes, both conducted by Beecham. As this was a political as much as a musical visit, the British authorities insisted that we play some new British music, and Britten's Sea Interludes were chosen; *Peter Grimes*, from which they are taken, had recently been first performed at Sadler's Wells, conducted by Reginald Goodall. Beecham, disliking and perhaps fearing all music later than Sibelius and Delius, refused to rehearse it, not even playing it through in Paris on the day of the concert. The orchestra, of course, had never played it. We practised our individual music, but had no idea what would happen when we played it together in the concert. What did happen was that Beecham conducted the wrong number of beats in the bars, the orchestra's leader frantically tried to lead and we floundered through and got to the end more or less at the same time. It was cacophony and the audience probably thought that the English had produced some extremely advanced and incomprehensible music during the war.

After the last concert in Paris, the orchestra went by night train to Brussels. There were no sleepers, so I climbed up on to a luggage rack over the seats and slept there – trains had nice, comfy racks made of a string mesh then.

Strongly against his wishes, in Brussels Sir Thomas had to stay in the same hotel as the orchestra, and one day, on our way up to our rooms, he and I happened to be alone in the same lift. To my surprise, this meeting terrified him. The little man, not now raised up on his conductor's podium, looked at his feet, lost his pompous self-assurance, shrank away and muttered something incoherent. Embarrassed myself because of his embarrassment, I looked down at him in his corner and talked about the weather. That evening, he was again totally at ease with his vast audience.

A few days later we got back to London, feeling like returned explorers, in demand for stories of foreign places.

Beecham continued with the orchestra for some time, giving as good concerts as ever, but I noticed how much he disliked accompanying soloists. He was bad at it and resented the attention being taken away from himself, and also I suppose it involved an unpleasant one-to-one relationship, like that with me in the Brussels lift. Years later, during a London rehearsal with Heifetz, things didn't go well. Beecham failed to keep up with the rapid violin playing, so Heifetz stopped playing, was rude to Beecham and made him look foolish. To get even with Heifetz, before the concert that evening Beecham gave a paper-bag of cough sweets to a back-desk violinist. During Heifetz's long solo cadenza, Beecham pretended to cough, made large gestures and whispered loudly to the violinist with the sweets, and the paper bag was passed slowly from one violinist to the next until at last it reached him. The audience was fascinated; and all attention was successfully diverted from Heifetz.

When Heifetz was recording with Beecham at Abbey Road studios, a group of journalists was asked to a session. During a coffee break Beecham said to the journalists, who were interviewing him and Heifetz together, "After the interval I shall record a Mozart concerto with Mr. Heifetz, the greatest violinist in the world," and then, out of the corner of his mouth, "That is so, Mr Heifetz, is it not?"

Conductors

Apart from a wartime orchestral trip to Dublin, of which I can only remember eating an amazing, astonishing, rapturously beautiful banana split in a snack bar in O'Connell Street – *real* bananas, *real whipped cream!* – life continued its routine in London. Overwork, exhaustion and a joke or two.

Exhaustion. If I said to friends that I was tired out after a day's work with an orchestra, they said, "Tired? Playing the flute? Don't be silly."

But just think what it involves. There's the sheer noise; any factory management would be prosecuted if their workers had to put up with the decibels that are routine in an orchestra. Later on, when I had a car, driving home after rehearsing Tchaikovsky or Shostakovich in a small hall, it seemed wonderfully quiet, the engine noise and the squeaks and rattles that I was used to in my old car had almost disappeared, for I was temporarily deafened.

Tiring concentration is needed in playing even, say, a Brahms symphony, which you know backwards. You have to split your mind. You scan the music some bars ahead of the actual sound, so you play, always from memory, music that you have learnt a second before. (If you look at the music actually sounding, you'll soon get caught out and stumble.) While reading the music, you keep fully aware (in peripheral vision) of the conductor, and follow his movements. You fit in with the bit of orchestra that is relevant, and you think of the effect your playing is having on the orchestra and the audience. And, most important of all, you check you're in tune with the other players every second and on every note. (Small adjustments to the pitch of most wind instrument sounds are made by the players' lips; this is done on the flute by blowing the air either shallowly across the embouchure (to sharpen the pitch) or more steeply down into it (to flatten it).)

Because of this divided attention, it's more difficult to play rapid music in the orchestra than alone at home. When practising, a trick I found valuable was as follows; first to play repeatedly a difficult passage so that it was fluent and comfortable under my fingers; then to play it several times more, but, while still looking at the music, concentrating attention on something out of focus just over the music stand: say a picture on the wall – the picture deputising for a conductor and causing the necessary divided attention. Orchestral players tend to be good car-drivers (unlike soloists and conductors, who mostly drive appallingly), for they can easily concentrate on the road ahead and be aware of events seen in the rear-view mirror and around them at the same time. Because they are trained to be aware of what is happening around them, they are aware also of other people's feelings, they become 'intuitive'. A player who is not aware of the feelings of others will fail as an orchestral player, fail to guess correctly the nuances of the player next to him, be too loud or too soft in chords, not blend his sound, and not follow small signals from conductors. I've so often seen talented, intelligent, but unintuitive players rejected by other players. "He doesn't fit in", they say.

Total accuracy and unbroken concentration are needed in the orchestra, and that's tiring. A slip in rehearsal brings titters from other players, an obvious slip in a concert brings gross humiliation, and several slips get you the sack.

In spite of the concentration needed, sometimes a rehearsal of a piece that one has played hundreds of times can be the most painfully boring thing I know. A three-hour rehearsal is a month in prison, and some concerts are worse. I swear that the New World Symphony lasts ten hours, and as for Tchaikovsky's Fifth, that lasts a day and a half; Johnny's, "Pretty bad piece; fifty minutes, even with a good conductor", must *surely* be an underestimate. Once, I got so upset with this hated, bombastic symphony that during applause for it I ripped up the flute part on the stand – and had to spend most of the next morning taping it together again. The Sixth Symphony is almost as bad, all banging noise or lugubrious depression; but the Fourth, because it has an entertaining flute part, passed more quickly, and it is enlivened by having in the last movement an endlessly repeated rhythm which goes da-da,da-da.DA;da-da,DA-DA, traditionally the words to which are "Stick it up your arse, Mrs Murphy." Not funny at first, but, after this has been said sweetly by the strings, loudly and pompously by the trombones and slowly and sentimentally by the oboe, every player repeating it over and over again, it starts first to be giggly and then gets out-of-control hilarious.

These are the players' words for the same composer's waltz in his Serenade for Strings:

> You should see when my girl makes water
> She can make such a wonderful stream.
> She's only the milkman's daughter
> But she will piss for a mile and a quarter
> And you can't see her arse for steam.

They fit the tune perfectly and have helped many a string player through a dreary rehearsal.

But nothing changes faster than what makes people laugh. The mere mention of certain banned words were funny not long ago, Shaw's use of 'bloody' in *Pygmalion*, for instance; or, I remember, a long joke about people in a fish restaurant, the only point of which was its ending with the words, 'Ah, sole.' In Aldeburgh there was an estate agent called FLICK & SON, and we thought it awfully funny to find one of his notice boards and join up the base of the L to the I. So *naughty*, it seemed then.

I'm glad that dirty jokes have died out, for I found musicians' ones, especially those with funny foreign accents, very tedious. Some short ones were better, though I didn't much enjoy those about what were then called 'nancy-boys', but I timidly laughed at them all the same. (eg Question: "What is the nancy-boy's idea of hell?" Answer: "A bottomless pit" – and that short joke *did* amuse me.) I used to think, "Don't these jokers have sex, as I do? Or if they do, why are they always *talking* about it?"

But jokes about the music we played were fun.

In the slow movement of Beethoven's Third Piano Concerto there's a long, slow passage for solo piano, followed by a wind chord which it is difficult to know when to play. Arthur, the flute-player with wife trouble, told me what to do. He said, "Wait until the piano slowly plays the rhythm 'have a banaaana', and then play." It worked every time.

Audiences probably think that conductors indicate players' entries to them, but that isn't part of their job. And, anyway, they are usually too busy with interpretation, not losing the place themselves, or just looking beautiful. Perhaps they have the fantasy that they are *playing* orchestras as they would play a piano or a violin. For instance, they often point at a wind player just as he starts to play, a totally useless gesture, for of course the player must pick up his instrument, take a breath and prepare himself, long before the conductor's indicating sign.

Bar-counting is automatic and semi-conscious, so you can daydream or even covertly chat to your neighbour and still play in the right place; and, if you know a piece, it's usually unnecessary except for extra security. But the Chopin piano concertos are nightmares of bar-counting for wind-players, and the music very easy to play, so much more effort is spent in knowing *when* to play than in actually playing. If, like me, you find these concertos boring, the next time you see one being played spend the time watching the wind-players and giggle at their glazed expressions.

When I was starting in the LPO, I was often doubtful about when to play, even in well-known pieces, and sometimes made dreadful mistakes. For instance, in the Colston Hall, Bristol, there was a performance of Beethoven's Fourth Symphony, which was broadcast live. I had never played it before and there had been no time for rehearsal, for we had been travelling all day and, of course, everyone else knew the symphony well. I made a wrong solo entry in the first movement and some of the orchestra followed me and some just played on, causing cacophony. Sir Adrian, suave as ever, saved the day. After a concert in which I'd made a mistake like that, I'd leave the hall by myself, ashamed and humiliated, but I gradually got to know all the usual pieces and, when I still made mistakes, became thicker-skinned, so that by the end of the war, when London became an international centre for music, I was fully professional.

From 1945, the LPO was for some years the English orchestra which played most often with the famous pre-war continental conductors: Furtwängler, Walter, de Sabata, Munch, Erich Kleiber, Ansermet, Koussevitsky, Celibidache, and so on. But not Toscanini, for after the war he conducted only rarely in England, and then only the Philharmonia, not the LPO.

Furtwängler was unpopular with the LPO because he was then thought to be a Nazi. Years later it was known that in fact he had not been and had behaved well, short of leaving Germany. Karajan was the bad one, but he was skilful at covering up.

Hitler wrote in *Mein Kampf*, 'We should never judge artists by their political views. The imagination for their work deprives them of the ability to think in realistic terms'. Furtwängler might have agreed with that, but not Toscanini or Casals or the many artist refugees from Germany.

The orchestra didn't play well for Furtwängler, not only because they disliked him as a supposed Nazi, but because they desperately needed training, and Furtwängler wasn't a trainer. He was used to the disciplined Berlin Philharmonic, not the ragged LPO, so he didn't even try to cope with our technical problems. There was an absurd performance of Beethoven's Seventh Symphony when, perhaps to compensate for the inaccuracies from the orchestra, he put in so much rubato that the music sometimes completely stopped, and, because of his vague beat, we didn't know exactly when to start again. He made disjointed movements, head flopping loose on the end of a long, scraggy neck, which I found disturbing and hypnotic. Tall, thin and bald, like an untidy Giacometti sculpture, he seldom beat to the rhythm of the music, but stood like a puppet on strings, fluttering his baton rapidly up and down. In fast music he sounded like a hissing steam train, spraying the string players near him with saliva. Boris, who had a beautiful and valuable 'cello, frantically cleaned acid spittle off the varnish during the concerts, while looking up and silently, vehemently cursing.

In a frightening performance in the Albert Hall of the Prelude and Liebestod from *Tristan*, Furtwängler conducted very, very slowly, with a total lack of precision, so the 'cellos never knew when to move to the next note and the poor wind-players all waited for someone else to play in their chords, none wanting to be first and alone. In the end someone had to play, and all the rest followed raggedly. It must have sounded awful and Johnny thought it the worst-ever performance, a good five minutes longer than usual.

I thought then that with his own orchestra, who had learnt to understand his odd conducting technique, Furtwängler must have got different results, for there was an impressive intensity about the man and his music, but he failed to get us to enter his trance-like state of mind. The newspaper critics said, more or less, 'Wonderful conductor, terrible orchestra', and we wondered how a conductor could be wonderful if the results were terrible. But then even now critics do tend to blame orchestras for bad performances and praise conductors for good ones.

Recently I happened to hear on the radio a recording of Furtwängler and his own Berlin Philharmonic playing the slow movement of the Eroica Symphony. It was hypnotically emotional and enthralling, but absurdly slow, and his orchestra was obviously as foxed by his beat as we had been in the LPO; a shambles, but wonderful – and no better technically than *our* shambles.

The LPO in the 1940s was indeed a worse orchestra than it had been before the war and very much worse than a super-efficient 1990s and later London orchestra, but some conductors drilled, bullied and cajoled it into very good performances indeed.

About this time the manager of the orchestra, Tom Russell, wrote a book about the recent history of the orchestra which he called *Philharmonic Decade;* but the older players said the title was misspelt and should have been written *Philharmonic Decayed.*

Soon after this Russell, a Communist, did the politically incorrect thing of visiting China, for which, amazingly, he was forced to leave his job with the orchestra. Some, such as I, disagreed with this sacking, but we were overruled by the vote of the majority.

Visiting conductors were given plenty of time, usually five three-hour rehearsals for standard programmes, so that technical as well as musical problems could be sorted out. Boult, Sargent and Cameron were given only one rehearsal for each concert, so we saw English conductors as unimportant and inferior.

The best orchestral trainer at that time was Erich Kleiber, the father of Carlos Kleiber. A little, bald Napoleon of a man, compact, paunchy and strutting, he had infinite patience in getting balance adjusted, chords in tune, bowings sorted out, phrasing exactly to his liking and rhythms taut and springy. With his amazingly analytical ear he could hear, for instance, a second clarinet who was a fraction sharp in a complicated chord, or one violin making the wrong sound-quality far away at the back of the orchestra.

Sometimes I thought him obsessively fussy – especially when he fussed over me. For instance, he asked me to play over and over and over again a simple two-bar phrase, the flute's first entry in Mozart's G Minor Symphony, and I never satisfied him. The two quavers were always too fast or too slow, there was always too much or too little evenness in the phrasing, the last note was always too long or too short, the first note too accented or too quiet. In the end I found it extremely difficult to play the phrase at all. I took this concentrated attention on me, and on this tiny phrase, to be like square-bashing in the army, a routine of discipline to get me into unquestioning obedience. But, although he was a sergeant-major, he was not malicious and he didn't humiliate the weak. No one disliked him, not even the cynical older players, but his concerts were disappointing. Without the teacher being able to instruct and urge us on in words, the vitality of the rehearsals was missing. We tried to remember what had been taught, but Kleiber seemed inhibited and almost embarrassed when forced to be silent and depend on gestures. It is a shame that none of his vivid rehearsals was recorded, though the LPO did make gramophone recordings with him and they seemed at the time to be better than his disappointing concerts. We recorded Beethoven's Pastoral and Mozart's G Minor, and probably much else which I forget.

After Kleiber, I found Bruno Walter dull and didn't like his soft personality, thinking him insincere. On the surface he was a nice, kindly bear of a man who waffled on endlessly during rehearsals about the inner meaning of the music. At least I think that's what he waffled on about, for by then, like the rest of the orchestra, I didn't listen to conductors when they got philosophical, and mentally left the rehearsal until the talking stopped. Kleiber's talk had been accepted because it was down-to-earth instruction about how to play.

But Walter gave an exciting performance in the Albert Hall of Mahler's First Symphony and a dismally sentimental one of Mozart's G Minor, so much inferior to Kleiber's, I thought at the time. (Recently I heard the recording that Kleiber had made with us then, and was able it compare it to a contemporary one made by Walter with an American orchestra. I was surprised to find that I much preferred the one by Walter, Kleiber's now sounding to me dryly unemotional and too fast.)

Part of the reason why I disliked Walter was because with him I lost self-confidence and played badly. I don't know why this happened with such a gentle person, for I stood up to bullies without much difficulty. As well as being bored, I was frightened of being inadequate for him.

In the 1940s the orchestra's most loved conductor was Victor de Sabata. Seen on the street, he was a little bald old man with a bad limp and a very pale, thin, lined face, like a sad, underfed Italian waiter; but after he'd made his way painfully to the rostrum and started conducting, his movements were like a ballet dancer's, his body muscular and agile. On the platform he was beautiful, with large, heavy-lidded, light-grey, shining eyes and a sudden glistening smile.

Like Kleiber, de Sabata was a virtuoso orchestral trainer, and he had such a memory that he never needed a score for rehearsals or concerts, and an ear that could hear the minutest detail, even in the loudest music. It impressed us that he knew scores in such detail. For instance, the second oboe was doubtful about a note in his part and said, "Mr de Sabata, please would you tell me what I should play on the second beat ten bars before letter C?"

De Sabata, without looking at the score, thought for a short time and then told him the correct notes.

He was immensely involved with the music he was conducting and would feel any inaccuracy or coarseness of sound physically. In a first run-through of a piece of music that I didn't know, I played a wrong note. This caused him so much pain that he doubled up, as though I had punched him viciously in the stomach. He stopped the orchestra and I cowered in shame at having hurt him and he scowled at me in the silence, gradually getting his composure back, and then he gave one of his amazing, glittering smiles, forgiving me.

He was usually quiet and gentle, addressing the orchestra as 'My gentlemen': "My gentlemen, please will you play pianissimo here," for instance. But now and then he would make a big scene, breaking his baton and shouting, though this was immediately followed by his great, disarming smile.

Although present-day orchestras are, as I said, technically very superior to the 1940s LPO, they seldom do what is the most difficult thing of all, which we were forced to do very well indeed, that is to play very, very, very softly. Some conductors such as de Sabata insisted on this and we simply had to learn how to do it. For instance, to play Brahms's written *pianissimos* really *pianissimo* is in some cases extremely difficult, and nowadays they are usually played safely *mezzo-piano*.

Unlike Kleiber, de Sabata not only got the orchestra to play with the utmost precision, but he would whip up performances to extraordinary heights of frenzy and, like Beecham, was best in short, exciting pieces. For instance, there was a performance of Wagner's Ride of the Valkyries in Bristol that really went over the top. At the end there wasn't the usual, immediate applause, but a stunned silence; a woman screamed and the scream was appropriate, and only then did the clapping start. Do we get such orgiastic performances of orchestral music now? I'm old now, and then I was young and perhaps more responsive, but I suspect that audiences greatly needed emotional music just after the horrors of war, and the orchestra responded to that need when it had a conductor who provided the drive. Today, there is less need.

With de Sabata, there were excellent performances of the standard repertory, such as the New World and Beethoven's Fifth, but the Eroica was beyond him. In trying to record it, he got the orchestra perfectly trained to be unanimous, perfectly rhythmic and correctly balanced; but the tempos and the interpretation foxed him. During these recording sessions, he became more and more angry with himself, more and more frantic. He cursed. He broke batons. He left us and sat alone in his room and listened to a Toscanini recording of the symphony. But all for nothing. De Sabata's recording isn't satisfactory (I heard it on the radio not long ago), for it lacks the musical intensity that was his speciality, and the tempos are odd and unconvincing.

In spite of that failure in Beethoven, he conducted a magnificent Ninth in the Albert Hall. I wasn't playing, for by then Geoffrey Gilbert had returned from being an army bandsman and we were taking turns in the first flute position, and he was playing on that day. I sat in the stalls and was overwhelmed by the music and by the power of the performance.

Verdi's Requiem suited de Sabata perfectly, especially the *Dies Irae*, which was an orgy rather than mere music. It's a shame that these magnificent performances weren't recorded, for we spent so many hours in preparing them and so much emotional energy in their playing, and they are all gone for ever. We all loved de Sabata.

Geoffrey's return to the orchestra improved my life a lot, for now I had to play only half as often and the endless fatigue of the war years was over. He brought back to the orchestra something of its pre-war standard; being a great teacher, he got the players around him to play in a more disciplined way, and he was a superb player, always perfectly accurate and stylish, though I found his playing a bit cool – after all, he wasn't only my colleague but also my rival in the orchestra, so I was bound to be critical. I wanted the other players to like me best.

His devoted wife, Marjorie, and I would arrange together how to divide up the concerts between Geoffrey and me. She so much identified with him that she would say, "Yes, we would like to play that concert, but we'll be away playing in Manchester on the date of that later one, so I'm afraid we can't play then."

The orchestra did many concerts with the Swiss conductor, Ernest Ansermet. He was an earlier version of Pierre Boulez; another 'neuter computer', as Boulez was called. He had been trained as a mathematician, not a musician, and it showed. Like Boulez, he was a pleasant-mannered man and was coolly detached from people and music; boring when he played the classics, but we enjoyed the way he got us to play Stravinsky. He spent most of his working life with the Suisse Romande Orchestra, which was no better than second-rate, and perhaps that suited him.

Players see conductors as either perfect or dreadful, and are often proved wrong in their judgement. For instance, in 1946 the LPO went to Walthamstow Town Hall to rehearse for a concert there that evening, but the conductor was ill. At first no one could be found to replace him, but eventually the orchestra was told of a promising young American conductor who was in London, and that evening a very handsome, dark-haired young man turned up, too late to do any rehearsing. The concert started with Walton's 'Portsmouth Point', which has complicated time-changes; the newcomer conducted faultlessly and we were all impressed. In the concert interval he chatted with the orchestra, showing an overpowering, all-American college-boy charm. Because he seemed so competent and pleasant, he was given more engagements, but his other concerts were a great disappointment, for he now seemed to us to be both inexperienced and untalented, so the LPO never engaged him again. His name was Leonard Bernstein.

A very jolly conductor was a fat, coarse Cockney called Charles Hambourg (Johnny called him 'the Stepney Slasher') who would hire the Albert Hall and put on popular programmes, and the crowds flocked in. On the platform, before the start of a concert, he would look around the hall, see that all the seats were sold, turn back to the orchestra, make a sign for money (rubbing together his thumb and first two fingers), wink and do a thumbs-up.

One of these concerts started with the Bartered Bride Overture, which begins with a syncopated rhythm after a silent first beat. He raised his baton to start, but couldn't raise the self-confidence to bring it down to get us going. Twice he tried again, but still failed. He stood there helplessly and then said in a strangled, petrified whisper to the leader, "START," and the leader got us all going with his bow, Hambourg joining in conducting a few bars later. After the concert he gave each of the orchestra a pound note as a tip.

People so often ask players, "Is a conductor really necessary?" and the answer isn't simple. An orchestra could play classical music competently and dully on its own. But there are decisions to be made if it's not to sound routine: exactly how fast, where to relax a bit, when to bring out subsidiary notes, why a chord is out of tune, and so on. These things have to be decided by someone (democracy in orchestras being too slow for so many rapid decisions) and the leader has too much else to do, but in a Mozart or Haydn symphony, although conductors are useful in rehearsal, in the concert they have little more to do. No player needs the four beats to each bar that are relentlessly given, so some become embarrassed at their uselessness and pass the time by acting a charade of their feelings about the music, usually looking merely silly. I wonder if it will ever happen that a conductor will be honest enough and brave enough at such (frequent) times and simply stand there with his arms at his side and listen to the musicians getting on with it. Improbable; I guess that most conductors take to their jobs partly because of being people with an unusually strong need to be in control, and to *show* that they're in control. Standing motionless would be a painful temporary loss of that show. Perhaps they think that they are *playing* the orchestra as they would play the piano.

But a conductor's job is to stir up the emotions of eighty or ninety hard-worked and probably bored people, people who have been working too much or who are worried about things other than music, and to make them feel the excitement and importance of a concert. That is what only the best can do, and trying to do it is what makes them behave in such very odd ways, quite apart from their individual madnesses. They have to make you feel that *this* music, *this* concert, *this* moment is all that matters. The best conductors somehow convince you that for the moment friends and foes don't matter, food and sex don't matter, politics doesn't matter; and not until you leave the concert hall does the real world come banging back.

Oboists and Others

The principal flute has his life enhanced or ruined by the oboe-player sitting next to him. He's there on your left almost every day, a friend or a constant irritation.

I've nearly always had happy relationships with oboists, and relationships is the right word; working so close together, both physically and emotionally, you're almost married. In nineteenth-century music the flute and oboe often play in octaves, so they have to blend and sing together, and this blending and singing makes a bond. You listen to his sound, adjust to his pitch and guess in advance how he'll play, for perhaps he has a tendency to linger on the top note of a phrase, or has an instrument that is, you think, fractionally out of tune on one note, and you have to adjust to that. Also, a friendly oboist, even more than the second flute on your right, gives you support, making a little under-the-breath joke if the conductor makes life hard for you, or saying a quiet and kind "Well done" after a difficult flute solo – even if sometimes only to cheer you up for not having played very well.

Jock Sutcliffe was an oboist I admired both as player and as person. In the College orchestra, where we sometimes played next to each other, he showed me what self-confident and expressive wind-playing should be, and his warmth of playing was astonishing. His playing of the oboe solo in the Benvenuto Cellini Overture was the best thing I ever heard at College. Later on we sat next to each other in the LPO during concerts with Kleiber, de Sabata, Walter and others, and he seemed so much at ease, just relaxing and enjoying himself, He played all rapid music without trouble. A flute is supposed to be more agile than an oboe, but for a joke he'd lean over to my music during rehearsals and easily rattle off passages that I'd had to practise. He was always pleasant and jovial, and probably was highly intelligent; I say 'probably' for, when young, his intelligence was hidden behind a difficulty in using words. I used to amuse myself by asking him simple questions.

"Jock, what time d'you think this rehearsal will end?"

"Well…Yes…Er…Er…Um…Well, I expect so." And then a roar of laughter. Later on he grew out of his verbal difficulties, and recently I heard him make a fluent and amusing speech at his own eightieth birthday party.

Another oboe player I liked very much was Terence McDonagh. Friendly and pleasant-mannered, he encouraged me greatly during my first days in the LPO, when I was lacking self-confidence. Like me, he had depressive moods but, unlike me, his moods worsened as he got older, and finally they ended his career. I find diffident, mildly depressed people more relaxing than very self-confident ones, so I felt comfortable with him.

During rehearsals he would talk as though he were doubtful whether he could manage one more note. "This is the worst reed I've used for years; I simply can't get any decent cane these days. What an appalling sound I'm making! I'm so sorry. It *would* happen just as I've got to play the *Tombeau*. You know, its just too bloody hard for me, and there's been no bloody time to practise". Then out would flow an apparently effortless stream of beautiful sound in Ravel's *Tombeau de Couperin*.

All this made me protective and kind to him, a player who was so much my superior in ability and reputation; and that of course raised my self-confidence hugely.

Also, he once said to me, "Playing in tune with you is as easy as falling off a log," and I was happy for days after that compliment, for he was a star and I a beginner.

Most oboists are worriers: the perfect reed that wears out just before the important concert, the pinching with lips and the high air-pressure, the squeezing out of little drips of air, the absurdly complicated and

Richard Morgan (Photo RA)

irrational key mechanism which is always going wrong, and the tiny octave-holes that for ever get clogged with water. They have a hard life.

But one oboist was non-standard. Richard Morgan was tranquil and totally lacking in neurosis. He played beautifully in the LPO and was always kind and helpful during the many years we were together. His relaxed attitude was infectious, so that when he was next to me I was calmer and more competent than with other oboists.

Some oboists, on the other hand, seem to be jealous of the success of other players, whatever instrument they play, and good playing around them is seen as a threat to their own security. So, sitting next to one of those, I was embarrassed to play well and fearful of unkind comments; but that kind of player was unusual, and they were so insecure that they became depressed if criticised by harsh and frightening conductors.

But, back to conductors.

Serge Koussevitsky, conductor of the Boston Symphony Orchestra, was in prospect very frightening, for we'd heard how his own orchestra feared and hated him; and, when he arrived, he was as formidable as his reputation. A little, bald-headed gnome of a man, with a violently red face, he looked bad-tempered and was even harsher than his looks.

His first rehearsal started badly. The two harps in *La Mer* were out of tune and he made a great scene, red face turning purple, saying that he simply refused to work with such an incompetent orchestra. He walked off the platform and sulked back to his dressing room. We were at first alarmed, but then we relaxed, pleased to be paid for having a rest. When he returned and showed that he was worth listening to, and that great concerts were in store, then we got to work. Some conductors make a scene at their first rehearsal, just to show who's boss, and this is usually accepted as part of their job, a ritualistic game.

Koussevitsky called us 'my children', thus emphasising our weakness and subservience, and as his children it was hard to see ourselves as adult musicians with opinions of our own, and therefore a challenge to him. The players reacted strongly to this treatment, some gazing at him, spellbound, in rehearsals and afterwards saying how wonderful he was; while others, such as myself, tended to be resentful of his manipulation. I thought, being keen on Freud then, that it depended on our early relationships with our fathers, and, as my father hadn't been a bully, I wasn't set up to love or hate bullying conductors. Boris, the handsome communist cellist, always either loathed or adored them with great passion.

Koussevitsky, like many very good conductors, seemed always to play music at exactly the right tempo, as though he had a unique ability; but I think that this is an illusion and is just part of a general ability to be persuasive. It seems to me that there's no such thing as a perfect tempo for music; tempos are different for different people. For instance, the old, functioning slowly, hear music as faster than the young do, and even two people of similar age may well not have identical perceptions of speed at different times of day; for instance, if I was in bed at three in the morning and I heard the Lilibolero tune that precedes the BBC World Service news, I heard a quick tune, but if I heard it on my car radio during the day, I heard the identical tune, but now sounding slower. Also, tempi we aren't accustomed to sound wrong; so, hearing a conventional tempo on the radio of a piece we've grown used to at an eccentric one, then we'll object to it.

We played Brahms's Fourth Symphony with Koussevitsky, and how can I describe what it's like to play a principal wind part of a Brahms symphony with a great conductor? (Yes, he *was* a great conductor, in spite of my carping.) As a listener, I'm out of sympathy and unresponsive to Brahms. The rich sound and the repeated building to climaxes make me feel ill; but *playing* his symphonies was wildly intoxicating, surely so much better than merely sitting in the hall and passively listening.

Koussevitsky had many hours of rehearsal which were like the impatient drilling of stupid children, and the way he taught me in detail how to play the flute solo in the last movement of Brahms's Fourth, a passage which always put me into an out-of-the-body trance, stayed with me always, so that in all future performances I remembered what had been bullied and cajoled into me years before.

In a concert like that one with the Brahms symphony, when the whole orchestra is totally involved, I found that my concentration on what I was doing was so intense that everything else was obliterated. Every other activity that needs great concentration, such as a really good game of chess, a fierce argument, or reading an excellent and difficult book, all involve for me a less complete taking over of my mind than playing such a concert. There was a feeling of unusual vigour, for all one's resources were summoned up for this life high point. Sometimes the flute seemed not to be there any more and technical problems no longer existed; I, myself, with no barrier of an instrument, directly sang the music. All around, and, it seemed, inside me as well, there was the music; I was it, it was me. Varying my playing, sometimes blending, vibratoless, with the horns, sometimes dominating the other players for a few notes, then shrinking into the background under an oboe solo, singing out again at full force with my own sound resonating in my head, more vibrato here for a lush tune, straight sound again with the clarinet, and as quiet as possible in a final wind chord; all the time following every gesture of the conductor, for he's the centre of the world.

When in those trance-like states, as when playing the flute solo in Brahms's Fourth, I thought that my playing had been taken over by something outside of me and that I could therefore relax and watch with confidence while the technical difficulties were played without effort (riding a bicycle, you don't *think* how to do it; it was like that); or sometimes I felt I was directing my playing from outside my body, suspended above my head, or even maybe that someone in the audience was controlling me. Or I believed that a long-dead uncle was helping me (an uncle who had died young, years before I was born) and I was calmed by his imaginary presence. I kept all these phantoms to myself then, and now see them as curiosities from my past, no longer believing in their external validity. And it seems to me now that these experiences might possibly be appropriate for a pianist playing late Beethoven – but for someone merely tooting a flute in an orchestra, very eccentric.

These weird feelings usually followed the playing of music which needed extremely unnatural breathing; long holding of breath, extra deep breaths, quick gulps of air, too much oxygen. Over-breathing causes odd effects. But whatever the causes of these oddities of perception, I'd be ecstatically happy when they occurred, and afterwards I'd get a lot of praise from my colleagues for my unusually warm playing.

After the concert, the outside world is unreal, pallid and far away, and the only thing to do is to go to the pub and have a few beers with your mates, people still in tune with you.

Watching solo virtuosi, those who are ecstatically absorbed by their playing, I'd love to know what their private feelings are: are they of the same type as mine? Or even more bizarre? What goes on in the minds of those crazy-looking pianists, those closed-eyed, emotional violinists, those frantic over-the-top conductors? But, if they also have strange fantasies, it would be impossible to find out about them, for I expect they'd be as secretive as I was.

As well as the exciting conductors, at that time just after the 1939–45 war we worked with some ludicrous ones. The most ludicrous was Celibidache, who became, in old age, a guru of conducting in Munich. Students travelled across the world to worship him and to gain knowledge of his deep musicianship. When I played with him, he was a very friendly and accessible young man – and a truly awful conductor. He conducted the LPO on several tours around England, and during the long train journeys we'd get him to tell stories about his wartime experiences. He had, according to his account, won the war practically single-handed. He'd been in every battle, had by himself even discovered Hitler dead in his underground headquarters. Then we'd maliciously lead him on to tell even more ridiculous stories, all told very seriously – while we tried to control our giggles.

He had actually conducted the Berlin Philharmonic a few times, this wasn't one of his fantasies, and we enjoyed his solemn story of rehearsing them. He told us how the French horn had missed an entry.

"I say to horn-player, 'Horn, why do you not play?'"

"The horn-player he answer me and say, 'Maestro, I am most sorry. I could not play, for I was weeping.'"

He told this straight-faced, as a testimonial to the deeply moving quality of his own conducting, though to us, of course, it was obvious that the horn had missed his entry because of boredom, and then had made a joke.

He was a jolly young man and his concerts were full of surprises. He did little rehearsing and on the spur of the moment would make violent tempo changes during concerts, which kept us on our toes; and he'd get very excited, outdoing even Furtwängler in hissing imitation of

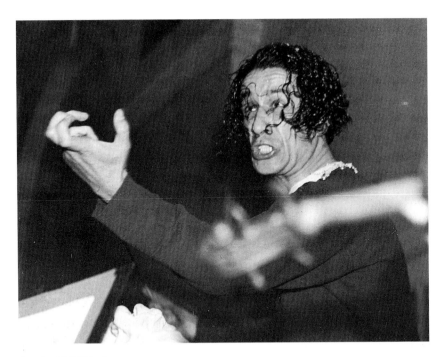

Sergiu Celibidache

steam trains, his face disappearing behind long, black, greasy hair. In the intervals of his chaotic concerts he'd drink a bottle of sea water (bought at Boots, the chemist, he told me) and then vomit; and after the concert he always went to the nearest fish-and-chip shop and wolfed down three portions of fish and chips.

If it wasn't an important occasion, and only a second-rate concert, we enjoyed orchestral chaos. For instance, a conductor forgetting how many loud chords there are and energetically beating one too many in silence, or trying unsuccessfully to get the orchestra to start playing again before the end of a soloist's cadenza.

In the middle of a cadenza to a Mozart flute concerto that I was playing on a live broadcast, Harry Blech twice tried unsuccessfully to get the orchestra going, but the orchestra just ignored him; and when the cadenza *had* finished, the orchestra started correctly while he was just standing there with his arms by his side.

Of course, the orchestra's own 'dominos' are hugely enjoyable, so long as they're not one's own. (A domino is when someone makes a very obvious, loud mistake, and best, a loud note played by one person between the final short chords of a symphony.) But, best of *all* is when a conductor gets in a muddle and beats a wrong rhythm, sometimes resulting in joyous cacophony.

In 1985 the RPO toured the USA with Menuhin conducting. In Boston, where we especially wanted to do well, André Watts was the soloist in Beethoven's Second Piano Concerto. The beat was so confusing at the start of the first movement that the orchestra all played at different speeds, and Menuhin had to stop the music and start again. This time we felt humiliated rather than amused. During another concert on the same tour, we were so confused by Menuhin during the last movement of Brahms's First Symphony that there was total chaos; nothing fitted with anything else and it seemed certain that the music would stop. We were saved by the horns taking charge and blasting out their notes, so that we all, including Menuhin, followed them, and the symphony continued. The newspaper next day gave much praise to Menuhin, but the horns were criticised for their over-loud, coarse playing.

The young Menuhin was an astonishingly good violinist. I first played in an orchestra accompanying him when he was in his early twenties; handsome and blond, his little hooked nose and unusual, wide-set, slanting eyes gave him the look of a wise young owl. I'd never before heard great violin playing, so his Brahms, with Henry Wood conducting, knocked me about emotionally.

That concerto is hard for the wind if Brahms's instructions as to soft playing are really followed, and the flute entry after the first-movement cadenza, a high note which must be very, very quiet and perfectly in tune with the oboe and horn, was stressful – but I managed it. (I often worried about playing high quiet notes, even though in fact I always seemed to play them all right.) After the concert I was on a high from the amazingly beautiful violin playing – and also full of pride at having played my own part well.

Nannie Jamieson, Yehudi Menuhin, myself, Eugene Cruft, Quintin Ballardie and George Malcolm

I wasn't so struck by his Beethoven. He'd played the Brahms on a rich-sounding Guarnerius, but he used a Strad. for the Beethoven, which was brighter in sound and to me less warmly emotional, and anyway, then I didn't like the Beethoven concerto much, for I hadn't yet heard a performance of it that showed me what it was all about.

A viola player in the orchestra (in fact it was Johnny the joker) who had played a few years before with the teenage Menuhin, said that now something wasn't quite right with the action of his bowing arm, which I, not being a string-player, couldn't detect – to me his Brahms had been perfect. I now realise that the tragic decline of his playing had already started. Only a few years later, I played in an accompanying orchestra with him again, and this time his control of the bow had gone, so that he simply couldn't play any short notes without a grisly scratching sound. He looked totally miserable; though in later years he appeared to ignore his inadequacies.

My opinion of that Beethoven concerto was changed by Ginette Neveu, for hers was the most intense violin playing I've ever heard.

She was a pleasant, friendly young woman: thin, brown-haired and masculine looking. She spoke English well and when we all travelled to concerts around England with her, we got to know and like her. She played chess with us on train journeys and chatted easily, and off-stage seemed to be a rather ordinary young woman. But when playing the violin, odd things happened. She stood very straight, not moving her body much, but the sounds were so intense that she gave the impression of demonic possession. During emotional music she'd usually close her eyes, but sometimes they would then open and, eerie and frightening, only the whites could be seen, the pupils having rolled up.

She played the Brahms well, and we were all impressed, but her Beethoven was in a class apart, and since then all other performances seem to me to be glossed over and uncomprehending. Parts of it she played very coolly, and then there were sudden outbursts of emotion, and it overwhelmed audiences, for I saw many people, like me, weeping. It was 1945 and the stress of the war needed release; this playing was the perfect channel for it. Nowadays, such emotional playing of classical music would be thought vulgar – and so much the worse for us.

There's a live recording of her Beethoven with a German orchestra, and although the playing in the first movement is more or less as I remember it, the rest isn't. Either she was off form that day or my memory of 1945 is faulty.

Johnny, who'd noticed the slight deterioration in Menuhin's bowing action, said he thought that Neveu's powerful bowing, the near roughness, would probably deteriorate in middle age into unacceptable crudity. But this forecast was never tested, for she died in a plane crash a few years after we knew her.

Another French violinist who played with the LPO then was Jacques Thibaud. As I said earlier, when I was a small child I often listened to his recording, with Cortot and Casals, of Schubert's B flat Trio, so I looked forward to seeing him, feeling almost that I knew him already.

At that time he was still only middle-aged, but he looked very old and sad. His technique wasn't what it had been, but his sweet-toned expressiveness was, and he gave touching performances of Lalo's *Symphonie Espagnole*, in which his violin spoke like a voice telling a story; but the quick parts were glossed over inaccurately.

He was a pleasure-lover, immediate pleasure that is. He was playing very badly at an orchestral rehearsal; he stopped, and to the conductor said laconically and slowly in his heavy French accent, "Too much fock." But in the end it was too much alcohol, rather than too much fock, that spoilt his playing.

Off and Away

Life was busy. Being in the LPO and playing as a freelance as well made any days off rare, so I wasn't spending much time at home in my pleasant, uneventful but sexually frustrating married life.

After living with Sheila for five years, I was humiliatingly caught out telling her a lie about where I was one evening. I'd told her I was working with Menuhin on a charity concerned with getting food to the post-war starving Germans, when in fact I'd gone for a casual sexual encounter among the crowd at Marble Arch's Speaker's Corner, then a place for quick and easy pick-ups. (After a nudge and a smile, male couples, strangers to each other, walked out from the crowd together and went elsewhere for sex.)

Sheila and I talked at length about my needs and my 'illness' and we decided that I'd have a Freudian analysis 'to cure me'.

In my case, the analysis lasted for eighteen months at four sessions a week. Whatever you think about the theory behind this sort of treatment (and nowadays I don't think much of it), repeatedly telling someone truthfully what you're thinking has a strong effect, and it changes you. But it's stressful, for what comes to mind is sometimes embarrassing, perverse, painful and difficult to say; but, like looking into a mirror, this looking at and displaying your own mind gives you a realistic picture of yourself. So I came to know more about myself, to know especially that my homosexuality was an integral part of me, not a disease, not a symptom of immaturity, and not something I wanted any more to change.

Near the end of this analysis Sheila and I went to France for a holiday, staying on a beautiful farm near Tulle, where we lived *en famille*, sharing the farmer's exquisite meals – those ceps in oil and garlic! There was fine weather and beautiful scenery and the two of us got on together amicably – but I was unhappy. Being with Sheila all the time for days on end caused greater tension than when we were both separately busy in London, where marriage was only part of life, where I could laugh and gossip warmly with colleagues, and have occasional stray gay encounters.

On the large terrace outside the front of the farm, with its huge view over the surrounding countryside, and just by our ground-floor room with its window open in the summer heat, each day a local woman with her little son walked together slowly this way and that. The child looked normal, but it never, never stopped screaming. Why it was suffering I don't know, but I identified with it, for I also was screaming, but silently, unlike the infuriating child. It hurt so much to be tied to a person I liked but who was of the wrong gender that I even envied the wretched child his overt screaming. Was I to continue in a half-committed married life? Telling lies when I had furtive sex? Continue feeling sad and guilty? I decided no, no, no I must not; so when we returned from the holiday I would have to end the marriage. However, I said nothing then.

Back in London I was unwell with a fever for a few days, and as I lay, hot, in bed I wondered how to do this awful deed of walking out on Sheila, the wife who loved me. A discussion wouldn't do. I would lose any argument and we would come to some sort of compromise, for she was so much better at putting a case than I was; I had to be brutal.

When Sheila was out of our flat I rang an old friend, Peter Graeme, the oboist, and asked him if he'd put me up for a few days. He agreed. Then, after having sex with Sheila for the last time, I coolly told her I was leaving.

I moved in with Peter and his Argentinian girlfriend, staying not just a few days, but three years.

After the marriage break-up, there was a time of mania. I was overfull of life, rushing about, having sex several times a week with different men, writing poetry, talking too much and too jovially. Cruelly it seems now, and insanely, when Sheila was out I went to the flat I had recently left, and covered the sitting room with an enormous number of flowers, filling every available vase, glass and cup. ("What was I up to?" I wonder now. "*Funerals* are the only places where you put flowers in that quantity.")

The subsequent divorce went through without fuss from Sheila, for which I was grateful, and perhaps she saw my unkind sudden departure as evidence that I was a pretty unpleasant character, not worth hankering after. She needed money while she trained as a doctor, which of course I gave her, and she later wrote asking me to stop it when she passed the final exams. Except for a couple of unhappy meetings, in both of which I showed a total lack of consideration for her feelings, I haven't seen her since.

I had known Peter (whose flat I had moved into) for many years, and had always liked him. He was most kind and considerate to me when we lived together, not apparently put out when I 'confessed' to homosexuality. For years we worked together in the English Chamber Orchestra and the Melos Ensemble. He, Inge, his wife, and I are still close friends, and their eldest child, now in his forties, is my godson.

Peter's flat, in 1948 when I moved in with him, consisted of a large studio, with a skylight, an internal balcony and a roof terrace, plus my small extra room with a separate entrance. It was right on the main street of Notting Hill Gate, but wasn't noisy because on the street side there were only a bathroom and a storeroom. This group of very pleasant and attractive studios was replaced by the present ugly 1960s block of offices and shops. Such a shame. My feeling of pleasure at living there was reinforced by a trumpeter from the LPO who came in for a drink one evening. "Gosh," he said when looking around. "Wonderful. This place positively *reeks* of sex". It was (also) perfect for small concerts and large parties, both of which frequently happened there. Although I was then twenty-eight, I wanted youthful jollity, for the very unjolly war years had been between my ages of nineteen and twenty-five, so I'd missed out on youth.

Ray, my viola-playing friend in the LPO, had a big Norton motorcycle. I bought a new Matchless 350, which he taught me to ride and service, and then I drove to concerts wearing white tie and tails, with the flute tucked inside my zipped-up flying suit.

But the hard work of playing in the LPO most certainly wasn't what I wanted then. There were the few excellent concerts, some of which I've written about, but I was gloomy about a future of playing mostly popular programmes in stuffy halls, simply blowing down a piece of tubing. So, soon after leaving Sheila, I also left the LPO.

The war was past. Marriage was past. Tchaikovsky symphonies were past. I felt free to live as I wanted, free to travel abroad, free to be myself.

After five years of England in wartime, France was foreign and exotic (as it had seemed the year before when I went there with Sheila), and to be a writer was my idea of freedom; so the next summer I crossed the Channel with the bike and a small tent on the back of it and spent five months wandering around Europe. The British were then limited to £50 of foreign currency, but France was so cheap that I somehow managed to live on that for my whole holiday. The pound was strong, the franc was weak, and the French government gave tourists cut-price petrol.

In my tent I wrote half a bad novel, realized it was bad and threw it into a dustbin. For most real novelists the characters take over and the writing becomes fluent, but for me it got slower and slower till it stopped. The theme of it was to find out what would happen to someone if he fully believed in the existence of other people, not just as objects that impinge, but giving them the love that he normally gives just to himself. It was a story about the attempt to become adult and no longer a self-centred baby, something which was important to me then, and still is.

Just north of Paris, in the village of Valmondois, lived the Geoffroy-de-Chaumes, a large family, bilingual in English and French, who loved the arts and everything English, and who encouraged young English musicians to visit them. They had a family house in the village and also a semi-derelict château up a lane nearby where English musicians and music-students could stay, free of charge, during the summer, and it was there that I started my long holiday. We cooked on wood fires in the old and shabby kitchen and ate out of doors with an accompaniment of lots of laughter and lively talk.

I played tennis with Colin Davis, who was staying there, then a not very promising young clarinettist, and tried my hardest to beat him, but he was even more determined, and I lost.

Paris was a short motor-bike ride away and I did the usual sight-seeing; one trip there was made with an enormous girl cellist smothering me from the pillion, a breast each side of my shoulders. The Parisians were vastly amused and cheered us on our way.

Fritz Spiegl was at Valmondois. He was then a flute student, and later on became a professional flute-player and, later still, a well-known music commentator. He and I went on my bike to Zurich to visit a girl-friend of his and then on to northern Italy, making a circuit of the roads around Mont Blanc, then back north. Fritz was tough and stood up to the long journeys without complaint, even though motorbikes had no springs on their back wheels then and French roads were bumpy. It was freedom. It was adventure. It was all strange and foreign. And there was no conductor. If Fritz had known I was gay he might have been alarmed at having to share a bed with me (as was the custom for two men in cheap French hotels then), but he might also have known that I wasn't so silly as even to consider trying to have sex with someone so obviously unavailable; and he might have guessed what I was up to in Aosta, a town teeming with handsome men, when I went off for a few hours alone.

After more time in Valmondois I set off alone for the Mediterranean. Driving my high-performance 350cc Matchless at the great speed of fifty-five miles an hour, overtaking everything and feeling superior to the little French two-stroke bikes and the slow Peugeot and Citroën cars, I was the rich tourist with the latest technology.

In a few days I reached the Mediterranean and, with the permission of a local farmer, put up my tent by a beautiful, curving, deserted beach not far from St Tropez, a perfect beach marred only by the loud, coarse songs of numerous nightingales which sometimes kept me awake. I became homesick for blackbirds. (That beach is now 'developed', with parking meters, pizza shops and high-rise hotels.)

By the beach, apart from the farm, there was only a single, rather grand villa nearby. One day I saw a superb, flashy Delahaye convertible arrive there, and later that day the car's driver came down to my tent and spoke to me in halting English, and I replied in halting French. He said that the local farmer thought I was a Russian spy and that he'd been sent by him to investigate me. I soon convinced him that I wasn't, and we laughed at the absurdity of the idea. The investigator turned out to be Jean Marais, the star of most of Jean Cocteau's films. Although the very spirit of handsome masculinity on screen, he was in real life an effeminate man and not at all handsome, with that camp way of walking, a glide, with the hands bent outwards from the wrists. He was an amiable chap and took some trouble to teach me the crawl, which he swam with perfect style.

It surprises me now that I had an almost sexless time during that long holiday. It would surely have been easy to find other gay men in nearby St Tropez and Cannes, for I was adeptly promiscuous in England, but I didn't. The sun and writing and swimming and sightseeing were enough.

When I got bored with my lovely beach, I rode off to Italy, spending time in Florence and Rome; but as the autumn approached I considered my quick failure as novelist and began to think with longing of the flute again, of my musician friends, the exciting concerts, and even with pleasure of routine work. I then saw that orchestral work isn't all bad, and, apart from the over-exciting and stressful times, the routine involved is in some ways easier than for most; after all, the hours are shorter than those of office and factory workers. In prospect it seemed not all that hard to return to the boring rehearsals, the silly conductors and the often unattractive music, if only by thinking of the pay cheques to come after my very frugal life with tent and bike. I thought of returning to the muddled identity of the orchestral player, where you're admired for playing well and sought after and made to feel important by orchestral managements, yet at the same time are abused and made to feel inadequate and childlike by some conductors. I had to face a return to that as well.

There's a story about orchestral musicians' muddled identity.

Two pompous principal wind players from the BBC Symphony Orchestra were playing golf together, and an employee of the golf-course was rude to one of them.

The other said angrily to his colleague, "Don't let him get away with that; tell him who we are."

There was a pause, and the colleague replied slowly, "Er...*who* are we?"

Back Home

I got back to Dover on a gloomy, grey, windy day – bliss after five months of heat and sunshine. Hair bleached blond, face handsomely sunburnt, and so vain when playing concerts again that I thought audiences were staring at me in admiration.

I'd expected to return to unemployment, but the LPO had failed to find an adequate replacement for me, so I was welcomed back into my old job. (In the late 1940s there was a general labour shortage, and this included the musical profession.) Also I started teaching at the RCM, my old college, but that lasted for only one afternoon; I was given dull pupils and promptly resigned – my whole academic career lasting for only about four hours.

I was once again in a discontented, bored, sexually excited mood and so, back in the LPO, I was upset by the limited orchestral repertoire of those days. Trying to play the concerts solely as jobs to be done, thinking that fifty minutes of Tchaikovsky, for instance, shouldn't be all that difficult to put up with, I failed to distance myself from the music, so, much against my will, I experienced over and over again the despair and frantic energy of the Pathetic Symphony and the horrible blare and sentimentality of the Fifth; and rehearsing Beethoven symphonies yet again became almost more than I could bear.

Peter, in whose studio in Notting Hill I'd returned from France to live, was making an adequate living as a freelance oboist, so in 1950 I took the risk of trying the same on the flute and resigned from the LPO.

There was little freelance work in London then, few small ad-hoc orchestras and no 'sessions' (sessions being studio recordings for TV, films, BBC and what were then gramophone records). But there were lots of concerts for children, unpopular with us because they were poorly paid and often took place in gloomy old cinemas with awful acoustics. I loved to play to children, but these concerts were sometimes toe-curlingly embarrassing. For instance, in a huge cinema in the poorest East End, the conductor started the concert by announcing in his slow, upper-class accent, "Boys and gyalls, in the ebsence of ennotated programmmes….", and at once there was pandemonium; children shouted and whistled, boys left the stalls where they'd been segregated and harassed the girls upstairs in the circle, and it took ages for the teachers to sort all that out. In another concert, in a girls' school this time, Harry Blech caused a sensation by discussing Beethoven's Three Great Periods; and, in a boys' school this time, another conductor caused delight by telling the story of how a young man was so dejected at being turned down by the young girl of Arles (*L'Arlésienne*) that he climbed alone up into a high tower and tossed himself off.

For more serious music, however, there was Boyd Neel, amiable, ineffectual and pleasant to work with, and Harry Blech, irritable and ineffectual in rehearsal, but, from 1951, giving brilliantly lively concerts in the brand-new Royal Festival Hall. Audiences loved him and I loved playing with him to the large audiences that came to his concerts, especially in Mozart piano concertos when played by Clifford Curzon, Myra Hess or Annie Fischer.

Curzon's intense playing was popular with audiences, though he looked very odd when playing, his bald head rolling loose on a scraggy neck, as though it might fall off. One evening Sargent was to accompany him in a Promenade Concert in the Albert Hall, Sargent's territory, even though Curzon was even more popular than Sargent. Before the concert, Sargent in his dressing-room had the first oboe brought to him and said, "I'll give you a sign during the applause for the soloist, after he's played. When you see my sign, play a loud tuning A; that will quieten the audience down. We can't have clapping going on too long."

Myra Hess played all the Mozart concertos with one of the part-time orchestras I was in; gentle, sweet playing, and, especially as I'd never before even heard most of these concertos, this was a great experience. I loved Mozart more than any other composer then, and felt personal gratitude to him for the wonderful wind parts in those concertos. Like Curzon, Hess played always from music, never from memory, which wouldn't be accepted today from a leading soloist. She looked rather sentimental when playing and Maria Donska told me, and I'm sure she didn't invent this maliciously, that here and there in her music Dame Myra had written the words "Look up", reminding her, during sad bits of the music, to roll up her eyes and give a soulful look to heaven.

In the early 1950s there was great optimism, for everything was in fact getting better and better. Food was at last plentiful, there was no unemployment, new social services were available, and people in Britain had a new attitude of friendly openness which contrasted with the worried, tense togetherness of wartime. The Festival of Britain, on a site by the Festival Hall, had exhibitions showing a future of leisure and new opportunities. New music was being written and new orchestras were being formed, and there was exciting renewed contact with international musicians.

One of the new orchestras was the Kalmar (given that name by its founder to commemorate the ex-lover who had recently jilted her). Its conductor, Colin Davis, was great fun to work with, but he was then amateurish and fairly incompetent, and I didn't fancy his chances when he later turned from playing the clarinet to conducting full time; but I was just plain wrong, for he was intelligent and self-critical enough to transform himself into one of the best conductors around. He is especially good in Berlioz and Mozart, and early on I saw him conduct a uniformed Military Guards' band in Regent's Park in a performance of Berlioz' Triumphal and Funereal Symphony. Wonderful for me because of the quality of this very eccentric music, but also because of seeing gentle, civilian Colin ruling the uniformed military, a symbol of peace so soon after the war. He and April, his wife at that time, were a lively and friendly couple and I have never liked people more, never enjoyed more the meals, discussions and joviality in their welcoming house in Holland Park.

I had by then become totally nonchalant about playing music, seeing it as simply a pleasant way of making an easy living, not as something serious. The only other flute-players who might have been my rivals, Geoffrey Gilbert and Gareth Morris, were so busy in their orchestras and with teaching, that I had all the best freelancing to myself. There was a lot of solo playing: concertos in the Festival Hall, solo broadcasts, recitals and chamber music around the country. I played with an easy vitality and relaxed enjoyment which I think audiences liked, although sometimes, when I'd been too lazy to practise, I'd lose confidence and play very badly, but not often, and it didn't worry me. I was conceited enough to think that my playing was more enjoyable to hear than any others', and, even when not at my best, happy at being able to give audiences some of my own sexy vitality. It was so easy.

Although I did well in England, I never made the grade as an international soloist like Rampal or Galway. I had plenty of virtuoso technique, but my playing was either too casual and undisciplined, too emotional and uncontrolled, or I showed too obviously my utter boredom with the music I was playing; and, also, I thought that only orchestral playing was seriously professional and fully testing, for, in playing concertos, sonatas and chamber music, I thought I could get away with any shoddiness so long as I played with confidence, vitality and a beautiful sound, whereas in orchestras accuracy was essential and there were other professionals around who would criticise poor playing.

I'd try hard to play flute concertos well in the Festival Hall, for they were special occasions in a special place. For several days before a solo performance there, at the back of my mind, like a singing shadow, I'd hear the sound of the music I was going to play, a continuous mental solo rehearsal, and was told by Trinidadian Tom, who was living with me at that time, that I wasn't in the real world at those times, but was vague and forgetful.

Just before playing a Mozart concerto, alone in a dressing-room in the Festival Hall while the orchestra played an overture, with a spasm of nerves I wondered if I could actually face going out, still so much alone, on to the brilliantly lit platform; but of course, as in my first rehearsal with the LPO in Kingston years before, I knew I had to face it. I thought I had something of value to give, and was worried that I might fail to project my feeling for the music, that my fear might kill the vitality; then I remembered the first time I'd heard the Mozart I was about to play, that record of Moyse at school, and think, "This is what I've worked for, this is what I was *made* for." Then, walking on, smiling and bowing, confidence would return and the playing itself became all I was conscious of; agreeing now with Sargent's demand at college, I became a flute, not a flute-player. As the anxiety changed to perfect self-confidence, even to a feeling of power and dominance, the irrational took over. I felt that this simple early Mozart was great music and that it expressed the deepest feelings, that I was daringly taking risks in the phrasing, touching every heart in the huge audience, that the sound I made was a perfection of beauty, my virtuosity staggering to hear. I was loved.

Afterwards, I accepted praise from the orchestra blissfully and went home a hero, but gradually reality returned, even depression, and I said to myself as I lay in bed, "For goodness sake, come down to earth. You really *are* a bit of an ass to think your playing in that little concerto was so vastly important."

Sometimes, though, the feeling of power and control would fail to appear. Instead of happily showing off I'd know that the audience was bored, and I'd notice them reading programmes or shifting uneasily. Then the flute sound seemed to stay with me on the platform instead of singing out into the hall, and I had to tell my fingers what to do instead of their being under unconscious control. My loud notes were harsh and sharp, the soft ones thin, feeble and flat. This happened once when Colin Davis accompanied me in a concerto and I felt his contempt at my poor playing, and afterwards crept away to a pub and just got drunk, though often after such humiliation I would look for casual sex in order to get back my self-esteem, a temporarily effective strategy.

A few weeks after playing that Mozart in the Festival Hall, I played it again in Weimar, then in Soviet-occupied East Germany, with a German audience in the stalls, and upstairs in the circle only Russian soldiers, much resented by the Germans below. The tension of playing at the same time to these two antagonistic groups, uniformed military and oppressed civilians, appealed to my pacific longing for reconciliation. I played my heart out, feeling, as I so often did, that I was singing rather than just playing the flute, unaware of anything but the music and its power to calm hatred. Just sentimental fantasy? Maybe.

After that concert in 1957, which was with the London Mozart Players and Harry Blech, we played in a hall which surprisingly had survived in bombed-flat Dresden (with vast placards in the emptiness saying in German, "We thank the Soviets for the rebuilding of our city"). We saw queues for cabbages in the streets, and then later we had lavish food in our comfortable old hotel, another surprising survivor of the bombing.

From Dresden most of the orchestra returned home, but an oboe-player and I went on by train to nearby Prague, where we stayed in an excellent hotel for a week, where again there was wonderful food for us tourists – lashings of caviare and Tokay.

During this week we played on the Czech radio, accompanied by Jean Eisler, who'd been a fellow student with me twenty years before. After the war she'd married a Czech and moved to Prague.

At College I'd been intimidated by her because of her beauty, her intelligence and her superior musical ideas – I'd once dared to ask her to accompany me in a show-off nineteenth-century bit of silliness, but she'd said loftily, "I'm sorry but I just couldn't play that sort of music." However, she'd grown up to become friendly and likeable by the time we met again in Prague. And she was still beautiful.

Jean's Czech husband, Paul, an economist who had been in the West during the war, had, until a year or so before my visit, held a very responsible job in the communist government (economic advisor on foreign trade), but, to my surprise, I found them, with their two small sons and two lodgers, living cramped up in a workers' flat. He was by then a mere factory worker, a lathe operator.

Jean told me that, a few years previously, Paul's boss, and a good friend, had told him that he had become politically suspect. For his own safety he resigned from his job. Soon after that, a purge of the government (the infamous Slansky trials) took place, mainly of those who had foreign connections or who were Jewish, and Paul was in both groups. He himself told me that he'd heard on the radio former colleagues being tried and even confessing to crimes they couldn't possibly have committed; and then they were shot. His resignation saved him – briefly.

Through Jean and Paul, my oboe-playing colleague and I met many English-speaking Czechs. At parties, perhaps because a little alcohol loosened them, they were surprisingly open in their criticism of communism. For instance, I talked for some time with a man who ran a factory making computers (yes, computers in 1957). He told me, with much emotion, that he was bound to fail because it was government policy that a party member must be given a top job in all departments. These people in control were utterly ignorant of computers, and the result was chaos in the whole factory. Another man told me of the underlying economic mess that the Czech government was keeping secret; and yet another, a student of architecture, spoke of his anger and frustration at being prohibited from leaving Prague and visiting nearby Italy.

Jean's father was Lord Layton, the owner of the *News Chronicle*, a popular British paper then. The Czechs knew this and took note of it, not wanting the bad publicity of the recent trials to be resumed if the Eisler family was ill-treated. So Jean was allowed to visit England with the two children, though Paul wasn't allowed out with them.

A few years after my Prague visit, the Czech regime eased up a bit and the whole family was allowed to leave together, and they went on holiday in Switzerland. A great day and things seemed to be looking up.

In 2005 Jean very kindly wrote for me the following account of the events that followed, to replace an inaccurate version that I had previously written and then shown to her.

"Things were slowly improving, moving towards what later became the 'Prague spring' of 1968. In 1965 Paul had spent four months lecturing at all the major American universities, he had also been called to New York as a member of the Preparatory Committee of the UN Trade and Development organisation (UNCTAD), and in the summer of 1966 he was invited to Geneva as a consultant economist to the Friends of World Peace Conference of Diplomats.

On this occasion Jean went with him. The Conference was a great success, and Paul was looking forward to returning to Prague to be professor and head of a new department at the School of Economics, and they decided to spend one day in the Swiss mountains before returning home.

They arrived late in the evening at Saas-Fee, put up their tent and booked a guide for the following morning. The next day they took the cable car up to the glacier, met the guide there and climbed the Allalinhorn, a snow-capped pudding-basin of a mountain, not very difficult to climb, but nevertheless a 14,000 footer and liable to be treacherous in bad weather. It was a beautiful day and only clouded over as they began to near the summit, by which time there was a wild wind and they were soon enveloped in cloud. At the summit the guide had just said, 'we won't wait up here because of the storm', and at that moment the lightning struck and the three of them (roped together) were hurled 300 metres down the mountain side by the force of the explosion. Sadly Paul – standing highest – had been struck and killed instantly – as was clear when they finally came to rest. As chance would have it, the accident had been seen by two other climbers who had walkie-talkie contact with the village lying far below. With great skill the guide was able to help Jean down (whose left side had been damaged and she could barely stand or hold a rope or stick) and as they came lower, far below, they saw the rescuers coming up to meet them with a stretcher. She was carried down to the hospital in Visp, while the others went on up to bring back Paul."

Eventually Jean returned to Prague with the two boys, where they continued their education. But now all three live and work in the West.

Friends and Lovers

One afternoon in 1950 I was rehearsing with the semi-amateur Kalmar Orchestra. Colin Davis was conducting. Peter was playing next to me, and sitting next to him was a tall, skinny young second oboist who had striped pyjamas showing below his shabby jeans, which in those times of more formal dress was even odder than it would be now. In the rehearsal interval Peter and I went to a nearby pub with him, and he turned out to be most likeable and entertaining. He was called Wynne Godley. I don't have a photograph of him but, when much later he became Jacob Epstein's son-in-law, he was used by Epstein as the model for the huge sculpture of Saint Michael outside Coventry Cathedral, so his looks are familiar to many. In the pub I learnt that, following a degree at Oxford, he'd won a scholarship which allowed him to study anything at any university, so, on a whim, he'd gone to the Paris Conservatoire and studied the oboe.

I soon got to know him well, and also his family – his mother, Lady Kilbracken, his brother John, Lord Kilbracken, and, closely for more than forty years, his sister Katharine.

For a year or two Wynne and I spent a lot of time together. He mixed very high intelligence with jovial sociability and, as with Malcolm Arnold, he freed me of timidities so that life with him became one long joke. Although not conceited, he treated waiters and servants as though he owned them, and he went to smart places in shabby clothes without embarrassment. With him I also had effortless social superiority.

In 1952 we set off together to stay at the Godley family house in County Leitrim, just south of the border dividing the two Irelands. We drove up to Stranraer and crossed to Larne near Belfast on a car ferry.

My car lost the use of its top gear on the drive up and had to be repaired in Belfast. "A couple of days to get the replacement part," I was told; so, at Wynne's suggestion, we left the car and went by train to Dublin.

"It's Horse Show week," he said, "so we're sure to meet people I know at the races, and they'll put us up."

As we went in to the race-track enclosure, the first thing we saw was two gentlemen fighting each other.

"Oh good," said Wynne, "they're people I know; one's Lord— and the other's the Earl of— ; one has gone off with the other's wife. Good to see them, it means all that set is here and we'll certainly get a bed." The fisticuffing gentlemen were separated and I was introduced to one of them, who seemed quite unperturbed by what had been going on.

Soon we came across a gaggle of Sloanish young English girls (then known as debutantes) and we joined them for chat about betting and racing form, though I don't remember actually seeing a horse either then or later. Among them was a very pretty, slightly older woman, also wearing her blonde hair long and straggly, the fashion then. She had a bruised eye. We all drank a lot of whiskey and I don't remember any more of the afternoon until getting into one of a fleet of ancient taxis and being driven slowly south out of Dublin into the Wicklow mountains.

The blonde with the black eye was called Lady Oranmore and Browne, and we were all going to her house to stay.

The next thing I remember is descending through woods to a lake with a pergola and a beautiful Strawberry Hill Gothic house, all white stucco, pointed-top windows and castellations. Behind the house was a romantic craggy cliff, perfectly suited to the period of the house.

We were met at the door by the butler, and Wynne, who had been eating bananas, put a skin on the step in front of the pompous-looking man, hoping he'd slip on it, but he calmly picked it up and solemnly showed us to our rooms.

It turned out that we had arrived in the middle of a party that had been going on for months and that our hostess's black eye was just a hazard of the revelry.

There were no Irish there, only rich or distinguished or aristocratic English, amongst them the painter Lucian Freud, whom I knew as Lux (pronounced Looks). We'd been at school together (where he was disliked for his cruel treatment of his riding pony). I used to meet him later in the pubs of Soho; he was friendly towards me, but then I was scared of him because of his reputation of being violent and having a thuggish gang to do his bidding. When Wynne and I met him in Ireland, he was married to Kitty Epstein whom Wynne married later, and then I heard gruesome accounts of her former marriage. She hadn't come to Ireland with him.

That evening the many guests sat at long tables for a very good meal. The drink was still whiskey, plus champagne when thirsty. With the drinking went lots of eating, laughing, shouting, boasting, flirting; and noise, noise, noise.

During coffee I wandered out alone onto the lawn, away from the house, under the beech trees, down to the silver-sanded beach, the full moon glittering on the lake, away from the brilliantly lit house – a house now like a little compressed box, bursting with people and activity. Comparing it with the calm night, I wondered, "Do I link with that noise? What am I? What's my life for?" Questions too vague to be answerable.

After breakfast the next morning, Wynne chatted to and liked charming Lux, and then the two of us got the train back to Belfast and my mended car, and drove on.

Killegar, Wynne's brother John's house, was also splendid, but run-down. A whole wing had collapsed the year before and was left to rot, and much of the furniture also was falling apart. You approached the house by one of two drives, each a mile long, and the house itself, built in the early nineteenth century, was set on a rise overlooking three lakes. I found that the food and drink provided were splendid and the house and wooded grounds were a world away from life as I knew it.

Wynne's brother John, our host, had recently been in Texas, where he had met a very pretty girl whom he'd impressed with stories of his Irish estate, even telling her that he'd give her a house in the grounds. How far he got sexually on account of this showing-off I don't know, but she turned up at Killegar with her fearsome mother to claim the house as promised and to claim him as husband. This didn't suit him at all and so he showed her several houses on the estate, all total ruins, and cold-shouldered her unkindly. The other guests were sorry for her, but failed to make contact because none of us could understand a word of her Texan accent, so she was left to moon around the house, looking miserable, while the rest of us gossiped, joked, drank and ignored her. I dare say that now we're all mid-Atlantic and can understand Texan, but not then.

The other guests included the jolly, extrovert Daphne, Marchioness of Bath, and Katharine, Wynne's sister.

Katharine and I came to be like loving siblings, so we could talk freely to each other and discuss our lives and our attitudes to religion, for she was devoutly Christian, while I gradually became atheistic. She believed in the validity of truth from faith, while I came to think of faith as giving no more than unreasonable beliefs either inculcated in childhood and then unquestioned later, or held for present emotional advantage. This disagreement caused no lessening in our friendship.

Through Katharine I again became friendly with Maria Donska, for they were close friends (but I'd lost touch with Maria for some years). At College we'd played some elaborate variations for flute and piano by Schubert, and we played them again at this later date in the Wigmore Hall.

After our Irish holiday, Wynne and I returned to London together and continued to see a lot of each other. After a very jolly evening together, we said goodnight, and he continued, "Oh, Richard, that was a lovely evening. What a pity neither of us is a girl and we could go to bed together," and we went our ways.

I had no sexual interest at all in him and was amused that this so heterosexual man could use such homosexual language to express his friendship. But later, when I realised that I shouldn't keep secrets from a close friend and I told him of my sexuality, this remark may have been remembered by him, causing awkwardness and a cooling of our convivial relationship. But we only gradually saw less of each other, and we still occasionally met. Close bonding between an openly gay man and a heterosexual one is difficult; both are inhibited, each fearing that any display of warm friendship will be interpreted by the other as a sexual advance. It's more difficult than a non-sexual relationship between a man and a woman, where rules of behaviour have existed for centuries. There aren't any rules for gay-straight relationships, homosexuality having been unacceptable until the recent easing.

Wynne joined the BBC Welsh Orchestra as their first oboe for a time, then abandoned professional music and went into industry, then to a job high in the Treasury, and lastly became a distinguished Cambridge academic economist.

At about this time, Peter, my oboe-playing friend got married and bought a house, and I went to live by myself in a room in Shepherd's Bush. After the conviviality of the last three years, life was rather lonely.

I had a bad attack of depression, partly because of the loneliness (in spite of a few happy friendships) but mainly because of my failure to get a really close relationship off the ground – lots and lots of sex, but always with men who didn't want to make a commitment, or with those I soon got bored with and didn't want to commit myself to. After all, picking up unknown people solely for their sexual attractiveness is unlikely to find you a good life-partner, and it isolates you from people in general if you treat sexual partners as bodies, not as whole people. It makes you harsh and selfish, even if you briefly feel very close and warm towards each person. But I found that this way of living had its good side, too. It was very exciting – the hunt, the danger, the capture (an enthralling, educational hobby) – and it gave me empathy with a large variety of people and taught me to recognise and to avoid the mad and the bad. This education and empathy were helpful for my future work as a Samaritan volunteer for, because of it, I more quickly understood people who asked for help, some of whom I would otherwise have found alien and incomprehensible, and I was good at dealing with and pacifying the occasional dangerously crazy people who came in to see us.

I was depressed also with being so self-centred, alone in an intermittently lively social life – lively with the help of alcohol and dexadrine (the latter lavishly prescribed by my G.P. when I told him, untruthfully, that I needed a stimulant to keep me awake when night-driving).

In 1951, long before discussing religion with Katharine and declaring my atheism, I still believed in horoscopes, palmistry, life after death, God, a soul separate from the brain, and that praying could alter the world.

One afternoon on my way home I was sadly driving alone down Ladbroke Grove and was stopped by the traffic lights at Holland Park Avenue. I stopped my gloomy thoughts and prayed right there, clutching the steering wheel like a prayer-book. "Please, please get me out of this emptiness. Please let me get to know someone I can help, someone I can worry about, someone I can concentrate on rather than on myself."

I'm not even now cynical about *this* sort of praying. I see it as setting one's own mind to be ready for future opportunities; I'm sure that prayer can sometimes change oneself but that it can't change the outside world.

My prayer was soon granted.

At that time I knew many young West Indians who had recently come to England. The men I knew were jovially sociable and carried over their light-heartedness into skilful and sensual sex. Unlike the gays I had previously met, they preferred to have sex with people they liked, not just with any desirable body. They also had the advantage for me, as I had a slight inhibition about having sex with people too much like myself (white middle class), that they were alien and I felt easy with them.

For a time I was with Jack, a handsome, amiable, jovial, silly chap from Montserrat. He lived in a huge house of letting rooms in Maida Vale, full of new immigrants. They were a friendly lot and I enjoyed the happy gossip, the dancing and the laughter. Urban Jamaicans laugh at 'small-island people' and they laughed at Jack's speech. For instance, one of them noticed that he said "goss-upping" for gossiping, and one day he reported gleefully when Jack was out, "You know what Jack said yesterday? It's not goss-upping any more. Now it's 'gossing up'."

Jack (Photo RA)

Then I told him, to his relish, what Jack had said about his decorating job "I put gloss paint on the doors, but on the *walls* I put *emotion*."

Jack was irritatingly feckless. At that time racial feeling was called the 'colour-bar' and I was keen to do what I could to help break it, and believed that bad behaviour by blacks harmed their cause. Jack, to my annoyance, told me that he was usually late for work, and once took a day off, "because it was raining". He wasn't worried about being sacked for there was a shortage of labour then, but it worried me that he was giving blacks a bad name. Because of this and because of his silliness, I slowly got fed up with him.

Jack's large room, which he shared with a friend, was a meeting place for others in the house, and one day there was a new young man there, whose name was Tom Pierre. He was very good-looking, his small face around huge and heavy-lidded eyes. He spoke with a fairly good attempt at an English upper-class accent. Unlike the others, who were content to work on the buses or in factories, he was here for education. He seemed a bit pretentious (or 'pretensive' in Jamaica-talk), so I gave him a little test. He came from Trinidad and I didn't know then what you called a person from there, so, instead of asking him in those words, I asked, "What's the adjective for 'Trinidad'?"

He answered without hesitation, "Trinidadian", and I then knew that he understood what an adjective was and that he had at least had *some* education and wasn't entirely a fake. We talked for some time without my having to use a West Indian vocabulary, and he was plainly very bright.

I'd recently met and liked a pretty girl (whose name I now forget) and, because of my failure to find anyone more promising than Jack to attach myself to, I thought I might have an affair with her (not bothering to think what this might do to her). She liked me and asked me to meet her parents, so I went to supper in Hampstead with them and we all got along amiably. After supper I walked alone for some way south down Haverstock Hill, where I'd lived for my first eighteen years, the house itself having been demolished long before. It was a pleasant winter evening and in the clear sky was shining an eclipsed moon and, walking down the hill from Hampstead, I gazed at the progress of the Earth's shadow. I reached the place where my old house had been and stopped, wondering what to do about the pleasant girl I'd had supper with. I stared up at the moon, thinking, "Shall I return to the correct life, the social acceptance, the pretence? I've got to choose NOW."

The eclipsed moon, and standing by my birthplace, made the moment seem like a fateful turning-point; and so it was.

There was a telephone box just there so, on impulse, I rang Trinidadian Tom and arranged to meet him. A few weeks later we were living together, first in my single room, then, when Sheila moved out

Tom Pierre in middle age (Photo RA)

of the Bloomsbury flat where we had lived our married life together, we moved in there.

Tom was good around the flat, altering the decor and making the place into a comfortable home. After a couple of years his student work took him to Dublin and then, as a houseman, to Coventry, but he stayed with me in the vacations and I visited him wherever he was and whenever I had time. We quarrelled often, but I was happy. He was the person I had prayed for, the person to care for, and I was able to help pay for his medical studies and generally to look after him. We made no pretence of being sexually faithful, but we were always best friends.

By living with Tom, or rather by having sex with him, we were breaking the law. This didn't apparently worry me, but I noticed that I was then taking an unusual interest then in books about life in prison (in order to educate myself for a possible future) and, when passing an ordinary policeman in the street, I would feel anxious and avoid his eye or would cross the street.

Tom worked hard to become a doctor and some years later, when qualified, he set up practice back home in Trinidad, where I visited him over the years for seven brilliant holidays.

He was a bundle of opposing qualities. Caring and loving: brutally unkind. Excellent, much-loved doctor: drunken, promiscuous layabout. Occasionally generous with large amounts of money: often absurdly mean about petty cash. Stuck-up, pretentious prig: intuitive, sweet-natured friend.

He made many enemies, but I stayed devoted to him, even though he often hurt me, and I was often shocked when he hurt others. He died in 1994, from a self-given intended drug overdose and in the last stages of AIDS. I was the sole beneficiary of his will, but as he was so deeply in debt when he died, I got nothing.

Noël, my mother, got on extremely well with Tom when he was living with me. They chatted, gossiped and laughed together, but privately she had her doubts.

"Don't at the end expect any thanks from him after all you've done," she warned. But when he returned to Trinidad as a newly qualified doctor, I was away from London, and he left a letter for me to find on my return. It shows only one of his many personalities, the genuinely sweet and loving one, a personality which his patients and I sometimes saw, but which he hid from most of his friends (although, I must say that this letter now seems to me rather like an embarrassingly sugary testimonial to my character). I showed it to Noël and it seemed to please her.

14th April 1961. My dear Richard, It is really very sad that you will not be here when I leave tomorrow. But I want to thank you for all that you have done for me during the past eight years. Above all you have been my best friend – but you have been sponsor, confidant, advisor, in fact nearly everything to me. May I repeat, Richard, that I am <u>always</u> conscious of the fact that without you my life would have been empty and worthless. You have not only made me a doctor but your influence has moulded my character. After all I knew nothing of art, music etc before I met you. Please accept my deepest thanks and appreciation. You may depend on my friendship at all times. I know that whatever I do for you cannot really repay you. What you have done for me is priceless.

I cannot help thinking that you are the only person with whom I have really been annoyed. Of course you acted many a time in a way that would normally annoy me but I was incapable of hating you even for a moment. This I think describes the depth of my feeling for you. I am sad to have to go away from you for such a long time but I hope to see you in 2½ yrs. Cheerio for now. You must continue to play as well as you have done – after all you must maintain your position at the top. I will try to emulate you in <u>my</u> field in Trinidad.

If I were unkind to you at any time over the past 8 yrs or if I annoyed you please pardon me. You know that I have only love and admiration for you. Goodbye, Love. Yours ever, Tom.

A few years after meeting Tom I got to know a Jamaican called Roy. His father had worked in the Kingston (Jamaica) docks and his mother had been housekeeper to Europeans in a large house in King Street (now a commercial street like Oxford Street, but at that time residential), where Roy lived alongside the white children. So, though generally uneducated, he learnt to play tennis and bridge and to like opera. We were seriously competitive tennis partners for decades.

After we'd been friendly for a few years, he went to Jamaica and then returned to England, married. Like me, he'd found promiscuous gay life unsatisfying.

Tom's kitchen in Trinidad. Roy on left. (Photo RA)

We still played tennis together in the summers and I got to know his young children. He then joined the RAF and in 1961 was posted to Germany, very near the Dutch border.

Finding heterosexuality oppressive, now and then he'd escape to Amsterdam, where he got to know a Dutchman. When Roy was back with his wife in Germany, this Dutchman had sex with a young boy and was caught by the police. Although homosexuality was legal in Holland, paedophilia was not, so the Dutchman was in trouble. To put himself in a better light with the police, he explained to them that he wasn't generally a paedophile and that he had a regular adult partner, and he named Roy. The Dutch police contacted the RAF police in Germany and Roy soon had an interview there with a pleasant-mannered officer, and it went like this.

"As you know," he said to Roy over a cup of tea, "homosexuality is legal in Holland, no problem there, but I think you'd better tell me a little bit more about what happened – just for our records."

So Roy told him.

"Well," said the officer, now harshly, "it may be legal in Holland, but it's certainly not legal in the RAF," and Roy was tried, sentenced to three months in military prison, then discharged from the RAF and sent back to England, where he was tried again in a civil court and sent to Brixton prison for another three months. His wife left him.

On leaving Brixton he had almost no money, no job, a prison record, and nowhere to live. Also, of course, he was deeply depressed. So he came to live in my house for some months while he slowly recovered. With my help he got a job and moved into a flat of his own, not far from me – and we continued our tennis.

Roy was one of those people who, without apparently doing anything, make you feel good about yourself, and I continued my (by then non-sexual) friendship with him until he died in 1989.

After tense concerts in the Festival Hall I'd sometimes turn up at his flat with a bottle, still wearing my white tie and tails, without him expecting me. I'd ring the bell, say who I was on the intercom, and always get his pleased, welcoming voice. "Ah, good. Richard, come *in*."

There would usually be other people there, for he was vastly popular – not only because of his pleasant character. He used to go to the local pet-shop and buy seed for feeding canaries, actually marijuana seed irradiated to kill it, and Roy found that the irradiation was not completely effective; so, when he planted a large enough quantity, he always got a good crop. The sunny west window of his sitting-room, on the third floor overlooking the street, was filled with the pretty, fluffy plants, and after harvest-time the leaves covered much of the floor, drying on plastic sheets.

When I visited him, Roy and his friends would usually be sitting around, drinking and smoking pot mixed with tobacco, and, as I can't inhale tobacco, for it rasps my throat painfully, I smoked my pot neat.

Roy caught the HIV, and for the last three months of his life was in a coma. On hospital visits the nurses said I should talk to him, not knowing whether or not he heard and understood. I talked about the pleasant times we'd had, about our holidays together in Trinidad, where I'd visited Tom so often and where he also had a close friend with whom he stayed, and about parties in his flat, about a visit together to Bristol, then I'd tease him about my winning at tennis, and so on. It's difficult to talk to a silent friend calmly, and sometimes I had to stop for fear of crying. Occasionally he made sounds, and once urgently repeated three vowels, the second one emphasised. They seemed to be the vowels of "I love you", though I wasn't absolutely sure. This isn't as sentimental as it first sounds, for he'd often said that I was his closest friend.

As happens to the old, many of my friends have died, some apparently closer than Roy. But I miss and mourn Roy even more than Tom, and continue a friendship with him in fantasy.

Musicians Remembered

Writing about life-long friends has taken me forward to my old age, but now I'll go back to the 1950s and the musicians I knew then.

British orchestras started to travel abroad as a matter of course, and there was a long European tour with the London Mozart Players and Harry Blech, a holiday for me because I had to play only now and then. The first concert was in Amsterdam, where all I played in was Schubert's Fifth Symphony; after that the orchestra did several concerts which didn't need a flute at all, so, while that was going on, I had plenty of time to drive across Germany and Switzerland and meet them in Milan for another performance of the same Schubert (a very 'good' (i.e. short) symphony by Johnny's definition). I enjoy driving and the roads were almost empty.

I'd recently bought a little car called a Triumph TR2. It was a bright, shiny pink and I felt grand and rich in it. It went much faster than most other cars then, and travelling at ninety miles an hour on the autobahn from the Dutch border to Switzerland, I was never overtaken. Going on to Italy, I stayed in Florence, going to pleasantly cool and empty museums and churches.

One day I had to get to Genoa for a concert, but found that the Mille Miglia car race blocked all roads leading out of Florence, so I managed to drive onto the route pretending to be part of the race until reaching a road going out of the city. The sides of the race route were crowded with people watching the cars and they cheered me on, mistaking me for a competitor, and, as the car's silencer happened to have broken the day before, it sounded suitably noisy and sporty.

After Genoa I stayed for several days in Siena and Assisi, rejoining the Mozart Players for the same Schubert symphony now and then. I walked about the untourist-ridden towns, spent hours alone with the Giottos in the empty Assisi upper church and stayed in rather primitive hotels. It was April, I had my open-topped car, and all Italy was new to me.

I picked up a pleasant young man in Florence, but then came across the peculiar Italian attitude to homosexuality at that time (and now, for all I know). Prostitution was so common amongst Italian gays then that it was thought that in every sexual meeting money must change hands; but in this case it was difficult for the young man, for he couldn't decide who should do the paying. We discussed this at length in French for he was a well-educated student of architecture, and my Italian consisted almost only of musical terms, and eventually I managed to convert him to the view, new to him, that sex didn't always have to be paid for.

Driving fast on the way home, I noticed a loud thumping noise whenever the car went over the frequent pot-holes of the then badly maintained French roads. Later, at a garage in London, I was told that the rear engine-mountings had broken, so the engine was weakly supported only by the exhaust-pipe and could have fallen into the road at any time, which might have been the end of me.

Soon after that, Dennis Brain, the renowned horn player, was killed when his car for no apparent reason left the road; it was a TR2 like mine. It had turned over and travelled backwards and upside-down so fast that the back of a rear leaf spring became embedded in a tree. Knowing what I do about my car, and knowing that a long scrape-mark was later found on the road where he died, I think his engine must have fallen on to the road, as mine so nearly did; the loosened prop-shaft then dug into the road surface and the car somersaulted. There was no official inquiry, and it was generally thought that he died because he fell asleep.

I knew Dennis quite well and liked him very much; he was pleasant and friendly, but reserved and quiet, unlike the traditional boozy and extrovert brass-player. He was a plump young man, with unusual, heavy-lidded eyes and, although quick-witted and intelligent, looked slow and simple. I worked with him often and enjoyed his playing enormously, for it was full of joy and vitality; but, like so many wind and string soloists, he did tend to play sharp. (Playing sharper than the accompaniment is a vice, but an understandable one, for it makes the soloist sound brighter and even more of a soloist. When upset by this uncomfortable sharpness, orchestral players say, ironically, "Better sharp than out-of-tune.") I think he'd have gone on from horn-playing to some other form of musical expression if he'd lived longer, for he was a competent organist and was interested in conducting, though maybe not ebullient enough to become a good one.

Like me at that time, he was obsessed with cars, and in orchestral rehearsals put car magazines next to his music, reading them whenever the conductor started talking. Before his TR2, he had a delicious pre-war V12 Lagonda, and I was overawed when he took me for a ride in this exotic but disappointingly noisy car with its multiple clackety tappets. (A few years earlier, at the age of twenty, I came across a V12 short-chassis convertible (that dream car) parked, unoccupied, in a side street, roof open, key in the ignition. I so *very* nearly jumped in and drove off. Gazing at the driver's seat, it was a hard struggle not to. But if I had, and had then been caught by the police, I would for ever have had a changed attitude to myself, seeing myself as weak and uncontrolled, rather than as flute-practising, serious, ambitious. I might even have become a drunken layabout. Quick, butterfly decisions can have chaotic long-term consequences.)

A younger horn player I knew at that time was Barry Tuckwell. He was fun to be with, full of jokes and good humour, and he sometimes made me giggle uncontrollably during concerts, which was embarrassing. All he had to do was to play in a subtly ludicrous style, or mutter a joke under his breath, and my own playing was blocked, for it's impossible to laugh and play the flute at the same time.

Tuckwell was jealous of Brain, so he tape-recorded Brain's solo broadcasts, keeping only the rare passages when the playing wasn't quite accurate; these he pasted together making a continuous recording of 'Brain-slips', which he gleefully replayed to his friends. Dennis was an accurate player, but he didn't value accuracy above vitality, as Barry perhaps did.

A soloist who had both the greatest accuracy and vitality was Jascha Heifetz. I'd listened to his wonderful records, so when I went to the Albert Hall in the late 1940s to hear him play the Beethoven Violin Concerto I expected something special and was shocked to hear him start out of tune and see his bow trembling with the 'pearlies'. He soon recovered his nerve, but, perhaps because of my recent hearing of Neveu's Beethoven, his playing seemed to me to be too cool.

Later on I played in a freelance orchestra conducted by Sargent for a series of gramophone recordings with Heifetz in Walthamstow Town Hall. The orchestra had the best violin section ever seen in London, with leaders and soloists even on the back desks, playing there just so that they could hear Heifetz. They were not disappointed, but each day he started by playing shakily, just as in the Albert Hall, and was insecure for a full hour, as though overnight he'd forgotten how to play; then suddenly he became the amazing virtuoso we expected. He recorded silly nineteenth-century virtuoso music and turned it into something grand and serious, and the virtuosity was uncanny, reminding me of how Paganini was thought to have been possessed by the devil.

On hearing the records later, I was disappointed; for although the playing was as brilliant and accurate as I remembered it, the devilish possession had gone. You needed to see as well as to hear him.

During the sessions I wanted to ask him what he thought when playing, whether he had similar odd experiences to mine, but it would have been impertinent, and have seemed plain crazy if I'd gone to him in between takes of a recording and said, "Mr. Heifetz, when you are playing, do you sometimes feel you're floating above your body? And do you think that a spirit of someone dead is playing through you?" Anyway, he was withdrawn and unapproachable, seeming to be off and away in his own world, not someone you could chat to.

The people at HMV records provided a car to take him to and from the sessions, and he complained to them that the chauffeur was listening to his thoughts and influencing him – so they replaced the chauffeur without comment.

His stinginess and eccentricity were famous. During those sessions I was told that, at his flat in New York, he'd recently had a series of rehearsals with Rubinstein and Feuermann. He suggested that next day, instead of going out to lunch, they should bring sandwiches, for that would save time. At the lunch break, Heifetz's butler wheeled in a large trolley on which was a four-course meal for him, which he ate in front of the others with their sandwiches without apology.

I was also told that when the then young violinist Kyung Wha Chung visited Los Angeles she arranged to see Heifetz. Arriving at his house rather early, she walked up and down outside and then rang the bell a couple of minutes after the arranged time. Heifetz himself opened the door, said, "Too late," and shut the door in her face.

Another odd character was Herbert von Karajan, who, I thought, crazily saw himself as vastly superior to the rest of humanity; but conductors often seemed to us players to be weird, inhuman creatures. In 1954, I went with him and the Philharmonia to the south of France and Switzerland, and the first concert was at Les Baux, in Provence. Before the concert, the orchestra was unwisely given a meal with unlimited wine; we were happy to relax after the long journey from London, the wine being much appreciated. After supper there were many strange sounds in that outdoor concert in the warm night surrounded by jagged rocky hills, starting with Jock Sutcliffe insisting on playing Scottish folk tunes instead of the usual tuning 'A'. Dominos were strewn and we just giggled and shuffled our feet. In my drunkenness I stared happily up at the stars, trying to force the apparently double ones back into singles. Karajan conducted, not with his usual closed-eyed rapture, but wide-eyed and surprised, perhaps the only time he ever conducted a concert with his eyes open.

After that, we went first to Aix-en-Provence and then to Lucerne for more disciplined concerts in the festival there. I was playing fourth flute, for I'd taken on the tour for the travel, not the music, and had time off for holidays as well as work, and even drove to Venice in my smart, new little Austin in between concerts in Lucerne with Karajan and Furtwängler.

I was in the minority in not liking Karajan's concerts, for he was the most admired, and expensive to employ, of all conductors then. He was a handsome, middle-aged man who showed off with flash young women in his flash pink-and-cream Studebaker, private planes and power boats. During rehearsals he wore a tight black sweater which displayed his thin and muscular torso; while conducting, he would look away from the score and gaze down sideways, admiring his own beautiful, undulating biceps.

I hated the way he smoothed out Mozart and felt that even in romantic music his supposed ability to create special sounds from orchestras was like a medical placebo, that people took the pill of the extra-high-priced seats for his concerts and imagined that special sounds were produced because of their price and because of his reputation and his evident dominance on the platform. Undoubtedly he was brilliant at manipulating people and he was always treated as king. He also knew a lot about gramophone recording techniques, so his records do sound unusually good, but I think that's because of his electronic skill rather than for any special sound that he got from the orchestra.

He was not abusive to us when displeased, but we were frightened of him all the same. I think that anyone who is very successful, very rich, very famous, very bossy and surrounded by sycophants is bound to be awe-inspiring, for that's how we social animals react, and we can't be at ease with such people. I think that the 'Great Man' is usually a myth. Some people have a talent for football, boxing, politics, conducting, the creative arts or being helpful in a saintly way. Those who have persistence in developing their talents (usually men, not women) and who are lucky in their careers have in common that they become famous. Once famous, others adulate (the need to adulate being built in to many people), and then the successful usually believe their adulators and behave in a superior manner. The superior manner causes even stronger adulation.

During a Karajan rehearsal with the Philharmonia in Edinburgh, a then famous young conductor called Guido Cantelli came in and sat down at the back of the hall. When Karajan realised he was there, he stopped the rehearsal and set about rearranging the seating of the orchestra. All the basses had to move, then the cellos, then the percussion. Cantelli stayed for an hour and a half, and during that time

Karajan avoided playing any music, moving the players about instead; as soon as Cantelli left, the rehearsal restarted. Did Karajan think that Cantelli would steal his conducting secrets? Could he have been scared of rehearsing in front of a young rival?

Later on, in London, I deputised in just the end of a Philharmonia gramophone recording session with von Karajan; Gareth Morris, the orchestra's first flute, had had to leave the session early. It was for Till Eulenspiegel, which I knew well, of course. There is one phrase in it which I found difficult to play; it starts with a very quiet high B, an octave above the clarinet, and one can so easily play it too loudly, not play it at all or be out of tune with the clarinet. As I slid into the first flute's chair I saw that very phrase in front of me. I got my flute out of its box just as the red recording light came on and, trying to be too quiet on a cold flute, failed to play the high note. Karajan stopped the recording and scowled. Another red light and another start. I played the note this time but it was too loud, and he stopped the recording again.

"No", he said. "No accent. Bring the note gently out of the air. Like this," and he blew on the back of his hand as though puffing away a feather.

As I sat there, feeling frightened and miserable, he turned with a shrug to Walter Legge, the boss of the orchestra, who was standing next to him, as though to ask, "How can I conduct with such inadequate players?"

While the orchestra watched and waited, Karajan and Legge both looked at me and smiled. I'll never forget those happy grins.

Freelancing

My friendship with Malcolm Arnold continued into the 1960s, but later on his increasingly malicious sense of humour frightened me; also, I couldn't keep up with his drinking, and was irritated by his linking of drunkenness with prestige and manliness. So, although we still saw a lot of each other when working, we were no longer close friends. I noticed that he became very good at relating to groups of people, but ill-at-ease one-to-one, happy with musicians he didn't know intimately, uncomfortable in his own sitting-room.

After jovially recording his Guitar Concerto with Julian Bream and the Melos Ensemble, this small group of musicians went to a nearby pub to celebrate. It was a shabby old place in West End Lane, near the Decca studios, but Malcolm discovered that there was some champagne hidden away in the basement – so he bought the complete stock. Pop, pop, pop. Everyone in the bar was given as much as they wanted; the news spread, the pub filled, and we all admired Malcolm for his generosity.

"Oy," said a local bloke, "is it always like this-'ere, 'ere on a Sa'urday?"

After that I spent a day in bed, vomiting, gaining no prestige or manliness.

Malcolm wrote some wonderful music for me, including three flute sonatas: the lost Northampton one, an unpublished atonal tone-row one, and the published sonatina. Most of wind chamber music was written for his LPO colleagues during the war, and, as well as the well-known Shanties, he wrote an excellent wind quintet which we broadcast once just after the war, in 1946; after that performance the clarinet player, Steve Waters, took the music home with him, put it in a drawer and forgot about it. It is listed as lost in the catalogue of Malcolm's music; but recently Waters died, the music of the quintet was then found, and it was given its second performance in 2002.

I didn't, of course, play in that second performance of the quintet, having long before then retired from playing, but from the 1950s on I played in most of his film music; he was brilliant not only at writing the music, but also at conducting the scores and getting on jovially with the session musicians. I was the piccolo player in his lovely music for a film called *Whistle Down the Wind*, a rather touching weepy about a young girl who thinks an escaped convict is Jesus and shelters him from the police. The piccolo plays throughout much of the music of the film and when I heard it later on TV was pleased with the sweet, melancholy sound I'd made.

Malcolm wrote two flute concertos for me, the second being the more exciting to play, but less catchy for audiences. In 1972 I recorded them for the gramophone, and they were reissued later on a CD, along with his other wind concertos. Malcolm was to have conducted the recordings, but he had a psychotic episode in Bournemouth, where the recording was to take place.

This episode was a grizzly comedy. He was staying in Bournemouth at the grandest of Grand Hotels, and had dinner there with the manager of the Bournemouth Sinfonietta, who later told me what had happened. In the respectable dining-room, full of blue-rinse old ladies, Malcolm suddenly stood up and shouted, "You old hags, this place is so boring." He then left his table, climbed on to the closed lid of the grand piano, stripped entirely naked from the waist down and danced to the hotel's background music. He was hurried off to bed, but woke everyone in the middle of the night by banging the dinner gong and shouting for breakfast. He was in hospital for some time after that.

Many years earlier, I'd visited him in Springfield Hospital during one of his breakdowns. It was a huge, dreary place and I found him in a large ward full of crazy-looking patients. He seemed well and was cheerful, but during our conversation he often laughed excitedly and I asked him why.

"Just listen to that radio up there," he said. "I don't know how it's allowed."

"Yes. But it's just an orchestra playing a waltz."

"But the words: they're filthy. How can they get away with it?" and he went on laughing at the words that only he could hear.

We were sitting on a very low sofa in a corner of the ward. He called out to a patient, an enormous thug of a man with red hair and a jutting jowl. "Joe," he said, "this is Richard. HIT HIM."

I looked around for help, but no help was available, so I just shrank lower on the sofa.

"Oh, come off it, Malcolm," said Joe; "you and your jokes."

In spite of being given the now discredited insulin therapy, Malcolm recovered quickly and came back to work, playing first trumpet in the LPO, but by that time writing music was becoming more important to him than playing it.

When older, he had more frequent breakdowns and during the last one was continuously suicidal. I was told by someone who knew him well (I think it was his publisher) that Malcolm then had a partial lobotomy (the front part of the brain being partialy severed from the rest), and from that time all his creative ability ceased. I asked his daughter whether this really had been done, and she strongly denied it; she is a psychotherapist and should know about such things.

I was also told, also by someone who should know, that Malcolm was deliberately given daily overdoses of his medication by people who would have gained financially by his early death, and that this overdosing caused his mental decline. I've no idea whether this is true either, and it's getting to be like the puzzle over Mozart's death.

Malcolm has lived for years with a devoted young man who treats him with great kindness, but he talked of longing for death when I visited him in the early 1990s. He was then silly and senile, with low vitality and no interest in the present except for an obsession about where and when his music was being played. When I was leaving, Anthony, his carer, said that Malcolm had been on particularly good form that day, for usually he became incoherent after being with anyone for more than half an hour.

In London I happened to meet his publisher again, who told me he had recently received a new score from Malcolm. It was total nonsense and obviously couldn't be printed.

Earlier on, he wrote a strange and emotional flute sonata for James Galway, who doesn't play it. "It's just a load of crap," Galway told me.

(An aside: Galway, when an extremely young man, joined the LSO. Before the start of his first rehearsal, the pompous managing director came across the already seated orchestra to welcome the new player. Galway stood up as he approached.

The managing director said affably, "Welcome to the orchestra, Mr. Galway, and please don't stand up."

"Och," said Galway, "I was only standing up to scratch me arse.")

When Galway was young he had lessons with many people, including a few from me, picking up a tip here and a tip there. I was impressed by his talent and enthusiasm and I liked him enormously. He's known as 'The man with the golden flute'; he has many gold flutes, most of them given to him by their makers. Gold flutes play better than silver ones – in the same way as gold watches tell the time better than silver ones.

I was once a judge at a BBC wind competition and we gave first prize to the young Northern Irish Galway, and this started him on his career. Among the competitors was a Southern Irishman who played very well, but not with Galway's flair. After the result was announced, the Southerner came up to me on my way out and angrily accused me of taking part in a Northern Irish Protestant plot.

"After all," he said, "I'm Catholic, the two South American entrants are Catholic, the three Frenchmen are Catholic and you go and give the prize to a bloody Protestant."

He was big and hefty, so when he held me by the lapels and said he was going to knock my block off, I was scared. However, he calmed down and did no damage. Years later he became a successful freelance player and we got on well whenever we worked together in sessions, and he did once apologise for his past aggression, blaming it on drink. We laughed it off.

As a freelance player myself in the 1950s I played of course in many film recordings, very many performances of Bach's B minor Suite and Fifth Brandenburg Concerto and even more of Mozart's flute concertos. There was much more live music on radio then than there is now, and early every weekday morning and late at night, there were classical music recitals. For the morning ones you had to turn up at seven o'clock for a balance test and then play a perhaps difficult programme when still only half awake. I would come out into Delaware Road dazed and stupefied, good for nothing for the rest of the day, and hoping that there wasn't anything more strenuous to play than a rehearsal of a big choral work with easy, inconspicuous notes for me.

Playing in a chamber orchestra was usually less exacting than playing in a symphony orchestra, but often more interesting musically. I was in the London Mozart Players, the Goldsbrough (which later on became the English Chamber Orchestra, which I was part of for many years) the New London and the Boyd Neel.

The New London flourished for a time but is now forgotten because it made no recordings. It had a tiny conductor who was married to an enormously fat Greek pianist, so he was known as 'The (K)Night on the Bare Mountain', after Mussorgsky's tone-poem. Which reminds me that the City of Birmingham Orchestra's conductor, Panufnik, was always known as Panicfuck, Blech was Belch, Munch was Chew, Mackerras was Macteararse, and a certain Scandinavian was never spoken to as Mr. Dreyer, always as *Herr* Dreyer.

Long ago these names stopped being jokes and became day-to-day usage. For instance, in the BBC canteen at Maida Vale I imagine this conversation taking place:

"Hullo Bill. I'm here with Belch. Who you with?"

"Flash this morning. Now it's Torture."

The information had been given that the first player was playing with Harry Blech, and the other had first been conducted by Sir Malcolm Sargent and then by the light music conductor, Sidney Torch.

Players like to rename their conductors, compensating to some degree for their harassment and oppression. But in the 1950s there was less reason for players to feel oppressed than there had been in the 1930s, or later on at the turn of the century, for there was no unemployment then and thus little fear of losing one's job. There was an acute shortage of musicians, and especially of competent flute-players, it seemed. Fixers of concerts and sessions would implore me to play for them. (Fixers are people who, for a fee, find and book players.)

"Please, please will you ask the conductor you're working for on Monday morning to let you off his rehearsal early so you can do my session at Elstree at two o'clock" or "Surely you can get out of that concert you're booked for next Tuesday? If you will, I'll pay you much more for mine." But I realised that it wasn't good for business to get a reputation for unreliability, so I usually refused these pleas. But the juggling with dates in my diary and attempting to please everyone took ingenuity and gave me a happy feeling of power and success. This fitting in of a lot of work was less difficult than it would be now, for it was so much easier to get around London in those days. When working at Broadcasting House, for instance, I would drive there through light traffic and usually park for the day right outside – and I can remember my irritation when once I found other cars there and I had to park a hundred yards away.

There was at that time a need for music, as well as a shortage of it, so a group of young players realised that there was a lot of mixed wind and string chamber music that was not being played, and the Melos Ensemble was formed. It was a group of five strings and five winds, plus harp and piano. Its first performance was in 1951 and I played in the group for nearly forty years, thoroughly enjoying most of the concerts, but sometimes finding the rehearsals painful. The clarinettist, Gervase de Peyer, took the role of boss, infuriating the others. He would state what speed the music had to be played at, which was disagreed with by Mannie Hurwitz and Cecil Aronowitz, and then there would be a long shouting match. To vent his irritation, Gervase would turn to me and say that my playing sounded bored and uncommitted (which it probably was) and that I had quite the wrong idea of how to play a certain tune. I would then accuse him of being too loud and too sharp, and he'd ask how I could know since I was gazing out of the window all the time and evidently not listening. The strings would then have a long conference about bowings in order to shut up the wind for a bit, after which at last we'd get down to playing for a few bars. Nearly everyone in the group smoked while rehearsing and no protest of mine would stop them (I'm no good at persuading people to do things), so I felt lethargic and ill and unable to cope with the violent musical arguments. At the tea-break we were all completely relaxed and amiable, talking musical and family gossip; but always we had to go back to the thick smoke and the shouting.

If I find myself dying of lung cancer, I'll know why, and if I cower into a corner when friends discuss music, again I'll know why. But, in spite of the rehearsals, we gave lively concerts, made good recordings and travelled about Europe together extremely amicably.

The larger the number of players in chamber music, the less suitable it is for democracy, the more violent and time-wasting the arguments. Our trios got rehearsed fairly smoothly; octets were battles. For instance, in a Melos rehearsal of Stravinsky's Wind Octet, in which we knew that the composer himself was to be at the concert, as the combative string players of the group were not there, I tried to be the one to argue with Gervase and tell him that he wasn't the only person who had an opinion about balance, tempos and so on; but the other players thought I was wasting time, so I gave up.

This performance of the Octet for Stravinsky and the rest of the audience was in the Hall at Dartington, and this tricky and difficult piece went well. It's often played with a conductor, but it's fine as chamber music.

Afterwards, during the applause, Stravinsky came on to the platform and shook our hands. A gloomy-looking little man, he surprised me by giving one of those limp, wet-fish handshakes. I've known others with that feeble handshake, and known them well. They are energetic and positive, not wet fish, but they have strong expectations of help, practical and financial, from their friends; they are users of people. (Truthfully, I haven't known enough wet-fish handshakers to be

Igor Stravinsky (Photo Douglas Whittaker)

absolutely sure of this, so maybe I'm making a theory too easily, something I tend to do.)

Stravinsky had just come from London, where he'd been conducting his own music in the Festival Hall. Because of his great meanness and anxiety about money, that concert had nearly been cancelled. During the afternoon he'd unexpectedly insisted on having his large fee in cash handed over before the concert, otherwise he would refuse to conduct. It was a Sunday and in those days, before cash machines, and the banks all being closed, this was quite a problem. However, the cash was scraped together somehow and the concert went ahead.

The Melos played a lot of the newest music, mainly in music festivals abroad, but also for the BBC. Much of this was enjoyable, for it's fun puzzling out new methods of notation, hearing new sounds and meeting young composers. But some of the music was just plain silly, or so I thought, and very difficult to play; but I soon learnt when it was necessary to play the notes as written and when to substitute an easier approximation, which usually fooled even the composer who'd written it. For instance, rehearsing a new piece in the Queen Elizabeth Hall, I had to play a long exposed passage for alto flute. It was very difficult as written, but easy if played with all the accidentals removed (as though using only the white keys on the piano). In the concert I played my easy version and checked discreetly afterwards for any reaction from the composer and Raymond Leppard, who was conducting. Neither had noticed anything wrong. Ray was embarrassed and annoyed when I confessed this to him later.

Once, in a rehearsal in Venice, I said to Donatoni, a fashionable composer of that time, "I'm sorry, but this whole page of your music is quite beyond me. It's simply too fast for my fingers."

He replied "That's fine, I want the effect of someone striving and failing."

That, however, was easy to do.

Also, during the same Venice Biennale, the Melos played a piece of music one movement of which consisted of only one repeated note, with successive instruments playing it. In the performance, after a few bars, it started to get difficult. The horn-player played a slightly off-key note, the violinist failed to play his harmonic correctly and I didn't play my note at all because I was giggling. We struggled on, but hilarity took over and eventually the conductor called the whole thing off, the audience never knowing they hadn't heard the complete masterpiece.

The Melos often played at the Edinburgh Festival. William Walton conducted us in his Façade. I cheated here too, for this music has top Cs for the piccolo and my rotten old instrument wouldn't play them, so I played B flats instead, and nobody heard the difference; the piccolo just shrieks incoherently on such high notes. Although Walton was an amateurish and physically inhibited conductor, he was pleasant to work with, for he was good-mannered and amiable. Edith Sitwell recited, an old lizard bedecked with huge jewels.

Mention of Walton reminds me of something that a flute-player at Covent Garden told me. He said that while Sargent was rehearsing

Walton's new opera, '*Troilus and Cressida*', Walton sat in the stalls. Sargent made a change in the flute parts, saying that the scoring was inadequate. There was a coffee break, and when the flutes returned to the orchestra pit they found written across their music, "Play as is. Fuck Sargent. WW".

After concerts at the King's Lynn Festival, the Melos were sometimes presented to a member of the royal family, which I found irritating. Surely, I thought, civil servants could do this job cheaper – and there are plenty of pop-stars, footballers and the very rich to fulfil the appetite for adulation. Meeting the Queen and Princess Margaret, I saw that they were obviously bored – and why shouldn't they be? – and that Prince Charles had a bumbling, forced affability. I once got stuck alone with Charles, neither of us knowing what to say next; embarrassing. But Queen Elizabeth the Queen Mother was a pro, apparently actually enjoying endlessly meeting new people. In those days my cynical opinions about royalty shocked and annoyed most people I knew.

On a very hot July evening in King's Lynn, during the interval of a Melos concert, the Queen Mother said to me, "Why do you wear that stuffy black tailcoat? Take it off and play in your shirt sleeves."

"But that would show off my rather unattractive braces", I replied.

"Well, take those off, too."

"But, Ma'am," I replied, "then my trousers would fall down."

"That would be fun," she laughed.

After another concert, Cecil Aronowitz, the viola player, was in a queue waiting to meet the Queen Mother and had got chatting to the man in front of him, a submarine commander, and by mistake they'd changed places in the queue. They'd all been sternly educated by a lady-in-waiting in the correct behaviour with royalty, especially that no one should initiate conversation or contradict anything said, so that Cecil, arriving out of turn, had to answer the Queen Mother's well-briefed questions about submarines – and he wondered later how the commander had managed.

Royalty takes me back to Sargent. He was a great snob. When he was the conductor of the BBC Symphony Orchestra he spoke to a second violinist in the interval of the first rehearsal after a winter break.

"How was your Christmas?" asked Sargent, unusually affable.

"Very quiet, Sir Malcolm. I just spent it with the family."

"Oh, so did I," said Sargent, and paused. "The *Royal* Family."

Jokes like that make me think that I'd made the right decision not to play so often in big orchestras then, but more often in small groups; but all the same I sometimes hankered after the rigorous technical expertise that's needed in a big orchestra. The symphony orchestra was where I'd been trained, what I was best at, what fully involved me. I realised that I was a simple-minded *player*, not a creative musician with ideas of my own; I was limited. So, in 1961 I rejoined the LPO. There was still a shortage of musicians in London then, and, paradoxically because of this, I was able to take a lot of time off from the orchestra, so the work was less tiring than when I had been in the orchestra for the first time. The more an orchestra needs you the easier it is to play less, for a much-needed player can always say, like a prima donna, "If you won't let me do what I want, I'll leave the orchestra altogether," and the management is so fearful of losing its best players that they have to agree. I did this mercilessly. I usually missed the opera season at Glyndebourne with the LPO so that I could play at Aldeburgh, for I disliked opera, finding it oppressive and demeaning being hidden away under the stage, and, when listening to it from the audience, wishing the people on stage would stop shouting and screaming so that I could hear the music from the orchestra. I also took time off from the LPO for long winter holidays, going for two months each to the West Indies, Ceylon and the Far East.

In 1963 I went to Trinidad for the first time to stay with Tom, who by then had a flourishing medical practice. Just before going, the violinist Mannie Hurwitz said to me, "The West Indies? You'd be mad not to take a camera on a holiday like that."

"But Mannie," I said, "that's the last thing I want to do. A camera round my neck like any old tourist? I want to look at things, not record them."

145

But he insisted, and even bought me a cheap German camera and some film, and when I got to Trinidad I was hooked, spending lots of time photographing the beautiful people and the scenery.

In those days, before television travel films, good holiday snaps weren't boring, so, when I returned and saw that my pictures were enjoyed, I bought good cameras and set up a darkroom in my house, and photography became a second profession, publicity pictures for colleagues filling a demand. Unexpectedly, photography made me see the world not more superficially, as I'd feared, but more vividly.

Tom looked after me excellently in Trinidad, even though he was so busy. He left me to explore the island in his posh new Humber Super Snipe, first on my own, and then with Jim, a very pleasant, handsome young 'dougla' (someone of mixed Indian and African descent). Jim surprised me by not knowing his own country all that well, so he was pleased to explore it with me. But he did know the names of the trees and flowers and which wild fruits were edible, which poisonous. We swam in little deserted north coast coves, drank in the local 'snackettes', chatted to the local people, and jovially ended each day in bed together. (In the late 1990s I visited Trinidad for the eighth time and was told that then, because of South American drugs and North American guns, it was too dangerous to wander off the beaten track as I used to do. "Best take the safe road to the big tourist beach now." Boring.)

I was in the West Indies for two months on that first visit, not only in Trinidad but all around the southern Caribbean. When about to go back to London I seriously considered coming back and settling in Trinidad for the rest of my life, though I don't know how I'd have earned my living. But I had the vague idea of selling everything I had in London (for only about £20,000, I remember estimating) and starting a business. I loved being with Tom, and I liked the warm weather and the easy, sexy friendliness of the people. But now I'm very glad I didn't return for good, but only for more holidays there – oh, those seven delicious holidays! – since life was so much more varied and mentally enlivening in London than it would have been in Trinidad.

I took my flute on those holidays and played occasional recitals and broadcasts, which to me were jokes and free of the stress of playing solo in London. Visiting tiny places, you were a celebrity. In Port-of-Spain, for instance, I was interviewed live on TV by a pleasant young man who asked the standard questions. "How are you enjoying Trinidad's rum and calypsos, Mr. Adeney?" And, "I expect the sunshine's quite a shock for you after the London fog."

I tried to liven things up a bit and was quite pleased with my clever answers. After it was over and the red light went off, a very distressed producer ran into the studio, saying to me, "My God, we forgot to give you a mike." So I'd been smiling and waving my arms about, but silently.

Later on in the same day, when playing music on the radio, the accompanist was so confused by the speed of the '*Flight of the Bumble-bee*' that she gave up and burst into tears, leaving me to continue solo. Tears for her, but a joke for me.

And a few years later, in Colombo, during a two-month holiday in Sri Lanka, a fan blew away my music of a Mozart flute concerto, leaving me to play on by memory. I remembered enough to continue for some time, but eventually stopped. I explained to the audience what had happened, we recovered the music and started the movement again. A friend afterwards commiserated with me for what he saw as my acute embarrassment; but, again, it was just a joke, well away from professional England.

London, especially, was musically professional, but so was Aldeburgh. From the end of the 1950s, and afterwards for many years I played at the Aldeburgh Festival, spending each June there, rehearsing and playing. We musicians rented seaside houses and had holidays, mixed with hard work. Benjamin Britten was the reason for both, but especially for the hard work; and even in long-ago concerts in the tiny, ramshackle Jubilee Hall, before the existence of the bigger Maltings Hall, it never felt like playing unimportantly in a provincial backwater.

Britten

I first met Britten in 1938 in the green room of the Mercury Theatre, after a performance of Auden's play, *The Ascent of F6*; Britten and my cousin, Brian Easdale, had together written the music for the play, though I don't know why more than one composer was needed. Brian (who later got an Oscar for his music for the film *Red Shoes*), told me at the time that they had composed together amicably, and that Britten worked amazingly quickly on his part of the music; for instance, when an Overture was unexpectedly called for, Britten wrote it in a few hours, without apparent thought. Brian was rather irritated that such a young, apparent novice composed so fluently.

At that time, Brian's wife, Frida, told me about an evening when she had had supper with Britten and Pears. "Benjie was so charming and amusing," she said, "but I wonder why he lives with that silly, fat young man, Peter. Peter just sits there, says nothing but platitudes, or is silent. He's so *boring*! But, mind you, when he sings, that's quite different. Beautiful! Has Benjie chosen to live with just a voice?"

My parents and cousins talked amiably and without criticism about Britten and Pears's homosexual relationship, which must have been very unusual in those days, and explained by their being on the edge of what was later called the 'Bloomsbury Group' of artists and intellectuals, who were famously free and easy about their sexuality.

Although I met Britten several times before the Second World War, I have no memory of any talk, only of his appearance as a very thin, lively, smiling man with thick, curly hair and a crooked nose, and, of course, for me aged eighteen, and so secretly gay, it was exciting to know that two young 'queer' lovers could live openly together.

Benjamin Britten (Photo RA)

(Not until sixty-eight years later, when I read John Bridcut's 2006
book *Britten's Children*, did I find out that in fact Britten and Pears,
although for convenience sharing a flat together in 1938, were not by
that time lovers. Their commitment to each other began in America
three or four years after that; so my relatives and I were quite wrong
about their relationship then.)

Peter Pears (Photo RA)

They went to America at the beginning of the war, and I didn't see them again until about 1950, when we met at lunch at the Holland Park ground-floor flat of John Amis and his wife, the violinist Olive Zorian. It was summer, so in the Amis's large garden the table for the five of us was laid on the lawn under the trees. Britten and Pears arrived rather late in their pre-war Rolls-Royce and I was curious to know what it was like to drive, and asked them; but they soon shut me up by showing their boredom with that sort of trivial conversation, and I became shy and tongue-tied. They had already begun to be a bit grand, and the three of us, John, Olive and I, felt we had to be extra pleasant, laugh at their jokes, and mind we didn't say anything to annoy them. And they were affable, like royalty in a good mood.

After they'd gone we felt like naughty schoolchildren when the teacher has left the classroom, and Olive told a story about them.

She had recently been to one of their recitals, and said that afterwards she went to see them in their dressing-room.

They greeted her with the greatest enthusiasm. "Darling Olive, how *wonderful* to see you. You are the one person we hoped would be here. How lovely..." and so on.

Then, during the chat, Ben said, "Peter, did you see that ghastly Ethel Bloggs in the front row? How can we escape her? *What* a bore she is!"

Soon the inevitable happened; there was a knock on the door and in came Ethel Bloggs.

"Darling Ethel, how *wonderful* to see you. You are the one person we hoped would be here. How lovely..." and so on.

Olive crept out.

I rarely saw Britten and Pears again until 1958, when I started to play regularly at the Aldeburgh Festival, and then soon got to know them pretty well.

At the end of his life Britten was Baron Britten of Aldeburgh, OM, CH, and, to me, even in his middle age, he was an aristocrat. I disliked thinking this, for I like to think that all people should be treated as equal, but I had to admit that his creative abilities, his performing abilities and his organising abilities put him into a higher class than most people, so I was forced to treat him as someone special. And, as well as admiring him, I liked him, for I was appealed to by his warmth, even though it was partly hidden by a fastidious timid quality, which said, "Please, please don't get too close," a barrier which must never be crossed. For instance, once when talking to him, to emphasise what I was saying I warmly put my hand on his arm, and he jumped back as though I'd put my hand on his cock. His whole body was private.

You want to bring grand people down a peg or two, especially if, as with Ben, you see that the grandeur is superficial and brittle; but when I criticise him or tell stories which make him appear foolish, it doesn't diminish my liking and admiration, for I sympathised with his battle between fragile conceit and that neurotic sense of inferiority which was so dangerous for him. The inferiority feelings and resultant depression sometimes got out of control and paralysed his ability to write music. (When I get depressed or manically conceited, I can say to myself, "Oh, come on, Richard, don't be so silly. You're just an average person; you can't be as low and despicable – or brilliant and successful – as you're feeling now." But Ben's fluctuations of mood were wider than mine and took over his whole personality, leaving no space for such self-criticism – and, anyway, he wasn't an average person.)

He over-reacted absurdly to criticism; the slightest adverse comment in a newspaper had to be hidden for fear of causing abject depression, and if I'd let him know that I disliked his music for *Death in Venice* and the Cello Symphony I would never have been engaged to play at Aldeburgh again. Luckily, I enjoyed most of his music enormously, especially when he himself was conducting.

He was surrounded by people who loved his music and who constantly praised him for it; condescendingly, he enjoyed sycophants and needed their praise. Once, after a concert which he had conducted, a woman knelt down and kissed his feet, and he didn't kick her in the teeth, or even look embarrassed.

Of course, not all creative people are like this. Sir Michael Tippett, for instance, with whom I've worked and have met socially now and then, gives a different impression. With him, I had no thought of our relative status and just enjoyed the lively talk and laughter. However, it does surprise me that the apparently simple and relaxed Tippett produced a more convoluted music than the continually worried Britten.

After a rehearsal for *Curlew River*, his first 'Church Opera', in which he'd been especially edgy, neurotic and demanding, I said to Peter, "Isn't living with Ben awfully hard work?"

"Yes it is," he said, "but it's worth it. At least I'm never bored – and what would I do on my own?"

Myself dressed a a monk for 'Curlew River'

Curlew River had more rehearsal time than any other new work that I have ever played. As there was no conductor, the tiny orchestra was not only taught to sing the plainsong for their entry and exit, but was also drilled into perfect precision for the complicated timing of the music. This all took ages. Singing so often the Latin of the plainsong, words that were a medieval plea for peace and tranquillity, I absorbed it and became peaceful and tranquil myself. Each day in my open car I drove from Aldeburgh to the rehearsals in Orford. I crossed the perfect Suffolk countryside in the perfect June sunshine, past the woods to the right and the flat fields down to the River Alde on the left, and on into the village. I walked round the church to the ruined Norman arches in the churchyard and stood by myself with an empty mind, feeling relaxed and happy. The eerie quality of the music, the singing of plain-chant, and the repetitive rehearsals, tranquillised me into an unusually quiet state. In time off, I took my new Hasselblad camera to the surrounding churches and photographed the monuments and carvings inside them. Sometimes the churches were almost dark inside and, because I was using slow film and small apertures for depth of focus, the time-exposures were as long as half an hour, and that slowness, that waiting with the open-lensed camera on its tripod slowly doing its work, while I wandered around in the sun outside or sat on a pew in a quiet, cool empty church, fitted in with the tranquil music of *Curlew River*, which still quietly played in my mind.

Peter acted and sang the Mad Woman in *Curlew River* intensely and didn't realise that he sometimes became highly ludicrous. Towards the end of that opera, she (or he) is confronted by the ghost of her young son for whom she has been searching throughout, and is ecstatic at apparently finding him. During the rehearsals, she made little camp runs and grabs at the young boy singer. I found this worrying, for *Curlew River* was in danger of becoming a paedophilic comedy; so I talked about my worry to Colin Graham, the producer. He too was worried and said he'd talk to Peter. Later, Colin told me he'd had quite a job getting Peter to cool it, for Peter thought the criticism quite absurd.

The three church parables (*Curlew River*, *The Burning Fiery Furnace* and *The Prodigal Son*) were played many times, and we often went abroad with them, for they are easy and practical for touring – a small cast, a small group of musicians, simple scenery; and they are played in

Britten hated being photographed (Photo RA)

churches, which are plentiful and cheap. In 1967 we took them to the World Fair in Montreal, which was a good holiday as well as enjoyable work. During a few days' break, two of us, Neill Sanders the horn player and I, hired a car and drove over the border into Vermont. It was the fall and we walked all of one day on the Adirondack Trail, through scarlet woods, not a British autumn tint in sight; up and up we went, following the signs on trees that marked the route of the Trail. We met no one all morning, and in the middle of the day, hot, tired and hungry, we realised that we were miles from anywhere and that there was no hope of lunch. We stopped at a spring and drank cool water, making do with that, glad for a rest in the cool sunshine. A couple of people with rucksacks appeared, going in the opposite direction, the only people we saw all day. The four of us chatted for a while; then they said that they had more food than they needed, gave us an ample lunch and went on their way. It was one of those magic days when everything is right. It was my first visit to the USA, and I was able to write home that I found the USA to be a rural country, backward, under-inhabited and under-developed. The next day we returned to bustling, noisy Montreal, then straight back to Britain and recording sessions with Britten.

The few players and singers needed for it made a gramophone record-ing of *The Burning Fiery Furnace* in Orford church, during which a TV crew with their bright lights were also making *their* record of the event. This TV bustle increased the already tense atmosphere and, during a recording break, Ben and I went to the pub by the churchyard for a pint of bitter, to get away and try to relax. Sitting quietly drinking his beer, he interrupted the casual chat and said that he was finished as a composer, that he had no more music in him, and spoke gloomily of his future as only a conductor and pianist. I tried to tell him how much I was moved by *Curlew River* and that he had no reason to say what he'd said, but he wouldn't be cheered up. He went on to write the three Cello Suites, the Third String quartet, *Death in Venice,* the Cello Symphony, and so on.

The War Requiem involved hard work with Ben in London during the many rehearsals for the first performance. He conducted the Melos Ensemble which accompanied the Wilfred Owen poems, and Meredith Davies conducted the orchestra and chorus. It was 1962, a time of acute tension, the year of the Cuba crisis, when it seemed that nuclear war was near; the plea for peace in the War Requiem was especially powerful at that time, and the plea was reinforced by its being played in the new Coventry Cathedral, next to the ruin of the old bombed one.

Peter Pears, in his intense singing of the Wilfred Owen war poems, and Heather Harper's superb performance, rang out in the resonant new cathedral like an appeal to people to live sanely and peaceably. It's a pity that Heather Harper didn't sing in the recording later on, but I can understand Britten's wish to have a Russian, Vishnevskya, a German, Fischer-Dieskau, and an Englishman, Peter Pears, singing together to suggest a resolution of international conflict.

Throughout the rehearsals of the War Requiem Ben was easy and relaxed, which wasn't usual when he was preparing his new works, and perhaps even he was confident that this one could not fail, and it didn't – though Stravinsky managed to be bitchy about it, saying that it was mechanically contrived, and talking sarcastically of listening to it "with Kleenex at the ready". This is the sort of comment that was, if possible, kept hidden from Ben, and I expect it was Peter's job to see to that.

In early 1963 we recorded the War Requiem in London, and straight after that I went off on my two-month trip to stay with Tom in Trinidad. During that time, sometimes even as an irritation, the sound of the Requiem would flood into my mind, even to the exclusion of the ever-present calypsos.

Peter in middle age was quite different from what Frida, my cousin's wife, had said of him when young, for he was educated and intelligent when I knew him, and not at all the tongue-tied, boring young man she had described in 1938. And he was no longer fat, as she'd said he had been. Life with Ben changed him, but he had a character totally in contrast to Ben's. Though some musicians feared him as the power behind the throne, I found him easy to get on with, and I liked him and admired his singing, which was musically sophisticated, technically assured, and had perfectly controlled intonation. He had considerable stage presence, but for me his singing was flawed by the too wide and slow vibrato (even less acceptable today than then). In about 1965, he took singing lessons which got it under control, and he sounded wonderful; but when the lessons ended, back came the vibrato as wide as ever. But, all the same, his singing was enthralling, especially in *Peter Grimes*, the War Requiem, and as the Evangelist in the Bach Passions.

Pears and Britten (Photo RA)

He sometimes seemed to be out of touch with the present day. For instance, he said to me, "I often feel that Ben should write an opera with a really *modern* subject. I think that an opera based on a tennis party would be ideal." After hearing Julian Bream play a delectable performance of Malcolm Arnold's light and charming Guitar Concerto, he said to me disdainfully, as though talking about something dirty and smelly, "Not to my taste. Really a little vulgar, I thought." And when Raymond Leppard organised a concert of Purcell songs and chose some rude ones – for instance, one in which the tenor sang, "My maid Mary has a thing that is hairy", and the soprano answered, "My man John has a thing that is long" – Peter was not amused, and Leppard wasn't asked to Aldeburgh again for some years.

The real power behind the Aldeburgh throne at that time was Imogen Holst, the composer Gustav Holst's daughter. She advised the Festival on programmes and had strong opinions on which performers should and shouldn't be booked. She had a forceful personality, though her ludicrous manner of a middle-aged woman over-acting the part of a Saint Trinian's Schoolgirl, made some people think she was foolish. She was not. I thought she should have taken up conducting as her profession, for in the little she did, she showed a great sense of rhythm, an ability to get to the heart of musical problems and a passion for music that was infectious. The ludicrousness would even have been to her advantage; it isn't chance that so many of the greatest performers are on the verge of being laughed off the stage. Just think of those superb, swooning cellists, those magnificent, screaming, gesturing sopranos, those tip-top conductors doing their absurd antics all alone on the rostrum.

Imo, as she was always called, had a gushing, over-enthusiastic way of speaking which could be dangerous. For instance (as told to me by the violinist, Olive Zorian), after a concert in Aldeburgh given by a singer, she and Ben went to the Green Room.

"Darling," she said to the singer, "you were simply superb. Exquisite. You quite sent me up to Heaven."

Then, when the singer was out of earshot, she said to Ben, "She really isn't good enough, is she; we simply *can't* have her here again."

There was a lot of this double-talk. Although alarming, even despicable, it was enjoyable as gossip, and of course we, the musicians employed at Aldeburgh, all made the most of it.

But, in spite of this, working over the years with Ben, I grew to love and admire him. He was sometimes cruel, neurotic, difficult, petty, and absurdly encouraging to sycophants, yet I was aware of a fearfully exposed person, unprotected by normal human toughness and insensitivity. It was as if his nerves were bare, so that what would be felt as a small discomfort by any normal person, was experienced by him as severe pain. Unlike most people, he couldn't turn off his attention and relax, so his senses were at all times assaulted.

His risk of pain could be sensed in his concerts. When he was conducting us, we, the players, caught some of his super-sensitivity so that we too felt the music super-keenly and worried more about the playing of every note. We also became neurotically attentive to tiny details of each performance. Although this was worrying, it was also enjoyable, for we were playing in excellent concerts, concerts to remember. Hard, but worth it, for Ben had the essential and unusual gift of the best conductors, that of making the orchestra feel that each performance was of the utmost importance, that nothing else in life mattered for the time being, and therefore everyone played with complete commitment.

I got to know him best during those long rehearsals for the church operas. In one of them, in which the flute-player has to play only the piccolo and alto flute, never the ordinary flute, there is a very high passage for alto flute which sounded unpleasant and which I disliked playing.

"Ben," I asked, "wouldn't it be better if I played these bars on the low register of the piccolo? They'd sound much pleasanter that way."

"No, no, no," he said. "Keep it on the alto. I want the sense of strain and difficulty" (reminding me of the similar occasion in Venice when Donatoni wanted an attempt and failure).

If, during a rehearsal for a new work, a player queried a note or anything else in his music, Britten would consult his score, rather than listen in order to hear what was right or wrong. He always refused to make any change, such as a suggested different dynamic for reason of balance, and stuck to what he'd written as though the score had been written by someone else and was sacrosanct. Conducting was a different mode of thought to composing, and he couldn't suddenly switch from one to the other.

He tended to write very difficult passages for the wind, skilfully knowing just how far to go, and then in rehearsal he'd grin maliciously at the struggling players. But there certainly wouldn't have been even malicious grins at any inaccuracy during a concert.

He was not only an excellent conductor of his own music, but was also good at a wide range of other music. He disliked Beethoven and Brahms, enjoyed some Tchaikovsky and some Schumann and adored Mozart and Schubert. He had a feeling for Bach, and his recordings of the six Brandenburg Concertos are full of vitality and joy, though they might not be approved of now, for genuine old string instruments were used (but with long necks and modern strings), and modern wind instruments, which can play loud and soft, instead of modern replicas of old instruments, as is now usual. The only bad playing is in the slow movement of the Fifth Concerto (with just flute, violin and continuo), for Ben unwisely didn't conduct this chamber music but left it to us, and we then played with ludicrously unstylish vibrato and rubato. I have only recently heard this awful recording (having not heard it when it was new) and I wonder what Ben thought when we were playing. He was perhaps too embarrassed to tell us to calm it. We are now used to the thin sound of modern 'original instruments' in Bach, so Ben's Bach recordings do sound a bit plummy, but good all the same; and they don't have the excessively romantic rubato and heaving expressive swells that many 'authentic' performances suffer from. They're now on CD.

Working with Ben, there was a total lack of casualness, of relaxation, but Peter was always there off-stage, bland and smooth, practical and sensible, providing the protective shell that Ben lacked. Without him Ben wouldn't have functioned. But a stranger seeing them together couldn't possibly see their great internal difference, for they both had the same conventional public-school-educated exterior. Neither was in the least effeminate in speech or manner, though Peter sometimes made me think of a conventional vicar's wife supervising the village fête, so perhaps after all there was something feminine about him, but with no hint of theatrical camp, either in movement or voice.

Ben's voice was deep-toned and pleasant to hear, his accent and into-nation like that of the present-day Prince Charles. He got on very well with children and, through his music, made close friends with many young and pretty boys. I know, partly from talking about this to two of these boys when they grew up, and partly because of knowing Ben to be a Christian with a conscience, that he never had a sexual relationship with them. It was all tennis, orange-squash, jolly jokes and first-name familiarity.

He was 'Benjie' when young before the war, and 'Ben' when older. During an orchestral rehearsal, an old percussion player, who had known him a very long time, spoke across the orchestra, calling him 'Benjie'. There was a shocked and horrified reaction, for it was like someone saying, when being presented to Prince Charles, "Pleased to meet you, Charlie."

He wrote an opera for television called *Owen Wingrave*, which was not a great success. It was recorded in the Maltings at Snape. The concert hall was turned into a vast television studio, and the orchestra was put right at the back of the auditorium, far away from the action on the stage. We sat for hour after hour in near darkness while the producer, the stage manager and the technicians worked things out below. Forgotten and ignored, an orchestra at these times feels inferior and wants to hit back at the superior people who have work to do; so, during these long waits, to make us feel better, the woodwind of the orchestra had a competition for making up rhymes about Aldeburgh people, the more sexual and scurrilous the better. Mine followed the current malicious gossip (the sexual part of which I knew to be untrue), but won the prize:

> There is an old fellow called Ben
> Who doesn't love women or men.
> His principal joys
> Are just thousands of boys
> (And Peter Pears now and again).

Ben and Peter always shared a bed, but some of their associates refused to accept their homosexuality. For instance, the oboist, Joy Boughton, who worked with them and knew them well, said to me, "I've heard the most terrible rumours about Peter and Ben. People are saying they're queer. Aren't people dirty-minded and disgusting! The very idea! We really must put a stop to all this malicious talk."

When I knew them later on, they didn't flaunt their love in public any more than most long-married heterosexual couples do, but to me they were so obviously married, and they didn't hide their closeness. This was brave, for they were breaking the law, and at that time some rich and famous homosexuals were prosecuted and imprisoned. In spite of the obvious obstacles against it, it was one of the most satisfactory marriages I've come across.

I played in many first performances of Ben's music, including the three church operas, two stage operas, (*A Midsummer Night's Dream* and *Death in Venice*), the television opera *Owen Wingrave*, the Cello Symphony and the War Requiem.

One piece I hated playing was *Death in Venice*. I found the music noisy and unpleasant and the libretto embarrassingly banal, descending, at one point, to Peter singing mournfully, alone on stage and for an awfully long time, what amounted to, "If you were the only boy in the world and I were the only man." I crossed out the title, *Death in Venice*, on the first page of my flute music, and wrote instead "Carry on up the Grand Canal", but someone soon erased that, I hope well before Ben saw it.

But the opera gave us what amounted to a holiday in Venice where we played a season of it at the Fenice Theatre – late-evening performances and all the days for sightseeing.

On returning to England we did some recording with the 'cellist Rostropovich, with Ben conducting, and I was puzzled by their deep attachment to each other. They spent a lot of time together, both in music and socially, yet I can't imagine two more incompatible types: Ben, quiet, reserved and critical; Rostropovich, excessively extrovert, an over-eater, an over-drinker and strongly heterosexual. Although I came across Rostropovich often, I never knew what lay beneath the bluster, though Ben must have found something worthwhile.

Rostropovich is famous as 'cellist and conductor, but his piano playing is also excellent. I went to a recital given by his wife, the soprano Vishnevskya, in Leith near Edinburgh, and he accompanied. He played the whole concert from memory, which amazed me, and his playing was superb; though I disliked his wife's singing, finding it too hotly emotional, loud, wobbly and hooting.

In Aldeburgh, during a rehearsal for the first performance of Sir Arthur Bliss's Cello Concerto, Rostropovich was the soloist, and, as the

Rostropovich (Photo Emanuel Hurwitz)

morning went on he got more and more agitated. Eventually he stopped the music, stood up, and said slowly and loudly, "I WILL <u>NOT</u> PLAY THIS CRAP." Ben, who was conducting, gently calmed him down, explaining how embarrassing a last-minute cancellation would be, especially as Bliss was Master of the Queen's Music; reluctantly, Rostropovich agreed to go ahead.

That evening, after the performance was over there was the usual applause and Bliss was called onto the platform to share it, whereupon Rostropovich hugged him, kissed him, and held him in his arms in apparent delight and gratitude. I was shocked by this two-faced behaviour, and at the same time maliciously delighted at seeing this famous man being so untruthful. But perhaps it was just all part of the necessary show-business façade of an international soloist.

Orchestras and Travel

In 1961, after ten years of freelancing, I rejoined the LPO, and it was less oppressive this time. I was older and a more competent, confident player, and the repertoire by then was wider, too, so less boring.

Soon, John Pritchard became principal conductor. Large, fat, amiable, with a camp voice which everyone imitated, he was always popular. Inside the fat man was a thin one, quite happy to stay there. The fat man was an affable gourmet, gentle and feeble. The thin one was intelligent, ambitious and practical, with a sharp verbal wit. He could make people look foolish, and with an acid word or two he did the job of bringing them to heel quickly and with minimum pain. The fat man suffered fools gladly, but the thin one ruled an orchestra without difficulty.

Very large orchestral forces, such as those in Richard Strauss and grand opera, suited him best, but not Mozart, which he made smooth and bland. But I did admire his treatment of touchy singers. For instance, if one sang out of tune in rehearsal, he wouldn't bluntly say, "That A is painfully flat; you simply *must* get it up to pitch," but, "Darling Mary, what you sang was simply superb – most beautiful. At the top of that lovely phrase, the A sounded just a *trifle* dull in sound. Do you think you could tighten it up just that teeny-weeny bit? It would be even more beautiful then" – and the next time she'd sing the note in tune.

At Glyndebourne, he conducted a Rossini opera for many performances. I was bored, and, in a little solo for the flute during an aria, parodied the soprano's style, using an over-wide vibrato and lingering absurdly on top notes. This caused giggles from the rest of the

John Pritchard (Photo RA)

orchestra at the time and a letter from Pritchard next day which firmly told me not to misbehave, a letter so brilliantly written that it couldn't be seen as heavy-handed or unreasonable. I do wish I'd kept it.

Unlike many good conductors, Pritchard enjoyed accompanying soloists, and he was good at it. I played a Mozart concerto with him in Germany, and the Nielsen in the Queen Elizabeth Hall in London; in the Mozart I was comfortable, but the Nielsen was a worry, for I'd never played it before. I played all the right notes, but in a rather inhibited way – better to play your first performances in small villages than in front of friends and critics.

Also with Pritchard, the LPO played several concerts with Claudio Arrau, the famous pianist. He was a quiet and self-controlled man, but, perhaps because of Pritchard's relaxing presence, during a rehearsal Arrau became entranced with one of the first violins, a blond young man. Because he was gazing so adoringly to his left away from the keyboard, he seemed to be hitting any old note, quite unlike his usual style of playing. The violinist, a conventional married man, was acutely embarrassed. "What shall I do?" he asked me after the rehearsal. "What's going to happen?"

"Well," I said, "don't do anything. He can't rape you on the platform in the middle of the concert. Don't be such a worry-guts."

There was no rape, but there was more gazing – and an awful lot of wrong notes.

The violinist Arrau liked the look of (Photo RA)

In 1962 the LPO, with Pritchard and Sargent, went to Australia via India, Ceylon, Singapore, Hong Kong and Manila. This was the first world tour by a British orchestra and, for nearly all of us, our first time away from Europe. Some were scared. For instance, one of the double-bass players hated strange food ("I'm bloody well not going to eat that foreign, Paki crap") so he bought tins of biscuits and huge chunks of cheese which he packed into his instrument case around the bass. At Bombay airport, the first stop, the Customs confiscated the lot as illegal, dangerous, foreign food.

On European tours, those who are scared at the thought of being away from home get drunk at the airport and then stay drunk; but on a long, world tour this is more difficult; though this time a few very nearly succeeded. Being drunk was, of course, seen as manly, the opposite of being scared.

The bus journey from Bombay airport to the city was overwhelming for a new visitor to the East. It was extremely slow, the bus pushing its way through a great mass of humanity in slums of the sort I hadn't realised existed. Everything was going on: people washing, people buying food, people sleeping, people urinating, people quarrelling, people eating, people, people, people. Safely behind the bus window, the journey was a quick education on what to expect in India. Eventually arriving at the hotel, near Victoria Terminus, I unpacked and then walked out into the comfortably cool evening air and sat on a bench on the seafront, feeling superbly relaxed after the long, noisy journey in our slow, chartered, turbo-prop Britannia. It was reassuringly like being on the seafront at Brighton. Two young men were sitting on the same bench with me and we got chatting. Like all Indians, except for the much westernised, they asked direct questions: how old was I? what was my income? married? and so on. I was amused and asked equally direct questions in retort. They talked as European men do when making sexual contact, so that's what I thought they were up to. I may have been right, but, on meeting other Indians later, I realised that their behaviour was standard.

I soon met many sophisticated Indians, mostly women interested in western music and involved in organising our concerts, and they, also, put me through a grilling of personal questions. Walking around Bombay with these richly-sari'd ladies along hot, crowded streets on sightseeing trips to temples and shops, I was amazed to see that, when confronted by beggars – and there were hundreds along the way, some with stumps in place of limbs, some with blind, suppurating eyes and horrible wounds – these sensitive, cultured ladies behaved as if the beggars were invisible; they walked straight at them, apparently not seeing the outstretched hands and appealing eyes, and continued to chat gaily about ragas and Beethoven symphonies. Incomprehensible then when there were no beggars in London, but now, with London's homeless, I find myself doing the same.

One afternoon the orchestra was taken by bus to the governor of Bombay's residence. We drove through the crowded streets past noisy, strong-smelling markets, little shops and hooting, jostling traffic (like the trip from the airport) until we arrived at a high wall with large gates, guarded by soldiers. Before the gates, the teeming, stinking masses; beyond them, an astonishingly beautiful, empty park leading to a silent beach. A few gardeners quietly tended brilliant flowerbeds; neat lawns were smooth and watered.

We played two concerts in Bombay, then continued eastwards. After a concert in Delhi, some of the players were asked to go to the Artists' Room to meet the Prime Minister, Pandit Nehru. Because of the crush of people milling around back-stage, only Nehru, Sargent and I actually got there at first, the three of us alone in the large room. Sargent and I were standing and Nehru was lounging in a low chair. Sargent was evidently very ill at ease and he started talking rapidly, telling anecdotes and laughing a lot, while Nehru, with a face like a tired, bored old spaniel, gave no response, just looking up wearily and letting Sargent get on with it. Tensely laughing more and more, Sargent talked faster and faster, telling funnier and funnier stories to his unresponsive audience of two, for I wasn't laughing either. Nehru continued to stare gloomily and rudely at him until at last other people crowded noisily into the room.

Not until years later did I understand why Nehru had been so ill-mannered: during the 1940s both Sargent and Nehru had been the lover of Edwina, Lady Mountbatten; first Sargent from 1941, then both concurrently while Mountbatten was Viceroy of India during the mid-1940s (Sargent visited them in Delhi then), then Sargent only after her return to England in 1948. I've heard said, though it seems unlikely, that Edwina and Nehru didn't actually have sex, but they certainly knew each other intimately. So Nehru knew a lot about Sargent, and, from the evidence of his behaviour after that concert, absolutely loathed him.

On leaving Delhi, our pilot obligingly did two low circuits of the Taj Mahal (so we could all say on returning "Yes, we *did* see the Taj"). We stayed for a few days in Hong Kong, and I explored the place on my own – for I found that sightseeing in a group reduces the impact of a place. I had an introduction to a gay English architect (just by being gay got one many useful introductions in those days, for we were all fellow members of an oppressed underclass) and he generously took me around the city, not only to the usual sights but also to the workers' housing he'd designed and to back-streets, bars and markets; also to a steam bath where the masseur skilfully and surprisingly caused me to have an orgasm by massaging only my legs, not usually an erogenous zone for me. I met many English and Chinese people, with whom we ate superb meals and went to jolly parties.

The LPO played the opening concerts of the then new City Hall, now relegated to second best to a newer one. In Colombo and Manila there were also pleasant social gay contacts, resulting in excellent sight-seeing from the inside, rather than as an outsider tourist.

After a concert in Manila, the American manager of Shell Oil gave a party for the whole orchestra in his magnificent garden, warm in the tropical evening. While we were chatting, he told a few of us how he had recently imported a Cadillac for his own use and how it had quickly disappeared. He reported this to the police. A few days later, the chief of police, whom he knew as a golfing partner, rang, sounding very embarrassed. "About your car, my friend, I'm very sorry indeed, but I have to tell you that your Cadillac is now the property of President Marcos. He fancied it."

On a later visit to Manila, this time with the English Chamber Orchestra, a few of us went to tea with Imelda Marcos in her garden, and she frightened me rigid. A surprisingly large lady, she dominated the little tea-party with her strident egotism, telling us all about her charitable work for the poor and her development of European arts in the Philippines. No one else got a word in. She talked with immense pride of her plushy new 'Cultural Center of the Philippines' on the seafront (near stinking slums). We'd come to Manila especially to play at this Center that evening. She and her husband, the President, arrived in a Cadillac, and she made a pompous speech in English to the audience, saying at one point, "After years of work and effort, I am extremely proud to open my new Center, this great suppository of Philippine culture."

On the earlier LPO visit we went on from Manila to Australia. In Melbourne, a double-bass player and I got to know some of the gay community there – and it was a community then, for they were suppressed and secretive. I went in a car with two others to collect a businessman friend of theirs who worked in an office building in the city centre. The sober-suited chap got into the car and said "How d'you do" to me. He closed the car window, then suddenly and alarmingly changed character. He screamed in falsetto, flapped his wrists and said in a camp voice to one of the Australian men, "And how's my lovely Mary?" I've an idea that camp carrying-on is caused by oppression, and this wouldn't happen in Australia now. There were wrist-flapping queens in Britain years ago, but now I think they only survive in TV sitcoms.

In spite of the puritanical attitude, I had no difficulty in finding a sex partner; unfortunately his parents came back to the house just after we'd got into bed and we had to get back into our clothes prestissimo.

Our Melbourne friends entertained generously, taking us on trips to the seaside and to parties. We got to know so many people that, on our last night there, the bass-player and I gave a party ourselves, borrowing a house on the Toorak Road and buying lots of good local sparkling wine. John Pritchard came, and got drunk with the rest of us.

In Sydney, the orchestra's two conductors, Sargent and Pritchard, stayed with the Governor of New South Wales in his residence, beautifully located behind where the Opera House is now. At a party he gave there for the orchestra, the Governor complained to me about Sir Malcolm. "That bastard! Whenever I go out he makes a pass at my wife. Thank Christ he's getting out of here tomorrow. If he wasn't, I'd slosh him one."

On the plane the next day, Sargent had no black eye, so he didn't have to put on more than his usual concert make-up that evening, and there was no scandal. Pritchard did, however, make the Melbourne headlines for his publicly stated objection to being refused entry to a country club simply because of not wearing a tie. It *was* the 1960s, after all.

Soon, orchestral players got used to world travel, thinking nothing of rushing across America and on to Japan, or flying to Hong Kong and on to Australia. In 1979, for instance, I went round the world twice, first with the LPO and then with the ECO. The ECO tour was with Daniel Barenboim, who worked with that orchestra often then. A secretive man, he hid strong emotions and great self-confidence behind a façade of giggling silliness. I was then contemptuous of him as a person, and he was contemptuous of me, both as person and musician. Being a conductor, he had the power to show his contempt. It's easier to love your enemies than to like the contemptuous, yet, in spite of the social discomfort and the feeling of musical inadequacy that he gave me, I admired him as one of the most gifted and inspiring conductors I've ever worked with.

The ECO played the Mozart piano concertos with him, a series of concerts of all twenty-four of them in the Festival Hall, the Salle Pleyel in Paris, and the Carnegie Hall in New York; then we recorded them all at Abbey Road. With Daniel at the piano, they were chamber music.

Daniel Barenboim (Photo RA)

Without a conductor, the musical bonding within the orchestra and the acceptance of his musical authority made performances that seemed perfect. He played best in large cities, for he fooled around in small, to him unimportant places; and, in recording, his intense communication with audiences wasn't there, often replaced by a facile schmaltz.

In New York he was at his best. To Europeans, at least to me, New York in the 1970s and '80s, except for a few new buildings, seemed to be stuck in the mid twentieth century: old-fashioned, slow and villagey. Shabby old subway trains ran slowly, traffic moved slowly, people even walked slowly, and service in restaurants was slow to the point of irritation. New York may have been a brash modern city in the 1930s, but not in the late twentieth century. The old-fashioned was accentuated for me by visiting friends in their charming nineteenth-century flat on Riverside Drive, like an old mansion flat in London, and by working each day in Carnegie Hall, built in 1891. As in Paris, people in New York are either bluntly rude or excessively polite, so you never know which to expect. That gentle viola player, Cecil Aronowitz, on asking politely at an international news stand on Fifth Avenue if they had the London *Daily Telegraph*, was harshly told, "Get lost;" then, immediately afterwards, asking a cop the way back to his hotel, the growled reply was, "Buy yourself a map, Bud." Cecil was highly amused. But, in spite of New York's peculiarities, I found being there pleasant and relaxing.

Daniel played all Mozart's piano concertos there with rapture and accuracy, and Isaac Stern played all the violin concertos scratchily and out of tune, but he made contact with the audience as though speaking to each person individually. He leant forward, pouring the music out onto the audience. Like Menuhin, although no longer playing well, he still communicated: the closed eyes, the rapt look, the skilful bullshit.

As well as Mozart's concertos, Barenboim conducted some of his symphonies. During the Jupiter, the performance was interrupted by a loud noise from the front row of the circle. Two fat cops were holding a man by the hair as they hit him on the head with truncheons. Into the genteel, Mozart audience he bellowed repeatedly at the cops, "You mother-fucking bastards. Get your cunts out of here." The music stopped and the bellowing went on. Eventually the man was dragged out by the cops and the Mozart restarted, although it was hard to concentrate on playing it. Afterwards, I asked a hall official about the incident. "Oh," he said, "the guy hadn't paid for his ticket," but of course I didn't believe him.

Barenboim and his parents in Switzerland (Photo RA)

In Auckland, New Zealand, I played a Mozart flute concerto with Barenboim conducting. I was scared that he'd make me feel small, but in the concert he was astonishingly helpful and intuitive in the way he followed my playing. Jackie du Pré, his wife, was in the audience, and afterwards, at an official dinner for the orchestra, I sat between them and found conversation slow and difficult. Ill at ease, I drank too much wine and told Daniel drunkenly that his talent was God-given and must be nurtured, which embarrassed him at the time and me the next day.

Jackie was a magnificent creature, tall, blonde, striding. Her vitality, both as person and as musician, was lovely to experience and her playing expressed unworried joy. Always pleasantly relaxed, she was chatty and friendly to the players around her. We liked her very much, so, of course, we were horrified by her slow disintegration caused by multiple sclerosis. During her very long illness she was in London and Daniel was living and working in Paris, and, reasonably enough, he took up with another woman there and had a child by her. Daniel often visited Jackie, but she never knew of this woman (whom Daniel married soon after Jackie's death).

I considered Daniel's conducting to be a mixture of very good and very bad. His interpretations were grand, with generally slow tempos, and he had that essential gift of the best conductors: making orchestral musicians feel that concerts were of life-and-death importance. Wonderful; but he didn't give clear preparatory upbeats, so chords often didn't start together. Wonderful, but chaotic. I think he actually *liked* the sound of an orchestra tumbling into a chord. Rather than the harsh precision of Toscanini, he admired the hot chaos of Furtwängler. I heard Daniel conduct Schubert impressively on the radio the other day, but I pitied the players, knowing their anxiety as they held back, each one not wanting to play first in those ragged chords.

In the 1960s, he conducted a series of performances of *Don Giovanni* at the Edinburgh Festival, and I was in the orchestra. Daniel was in superb control then, knowing every note and word by heart. He made the opera sound solemn and gloomy, which I thought right, but the critics hated his slow tempos.

In *Don Giovanni* the trombones don't play until well into the second act, and have the wait well timed. The mandolin also has to wait. There are many pubs by Edinburgh's King's Theatre, where we were playing. Trombonists are more used to alcohol than mandolin-players. The mandolin-player in the opera was a pompous and respectable gentleman, but he apparently wanted to be manly and keep up with the trombonists' rate of drinking, so, when he got back to the theatre and played his obbligato, he drunkenly let his emotions run riot; he must have thought he was playing with great beauty, for there were sentimental *rubati*, wrong notes, comically fumbled scales and a gradual slowing down of tempo, forcing the singer also to sing slower and slower. Barenboim was helpless. His beat was ignored. But the orchestra loved it, laughing noisily, hidden under the stage.

Although famous as a jet-setter, Barenboim wasn't pretentious or a social climber; he was too self-confident to need that sort of success. At a large supper-party given by a rich merchant banker in his big and gloomy South Kensington house, Barenboim and I were among the guests. After drinks upstairs in the drawing-room, we started to go down to dinner. He and I were among the last to leave the room and so we saw our immensely rich host painstakingly turning out the lights and switching off the electric fires. This parsimony amused Barenboim so much, and he was so splutteringly noisy about it, that the ECO manager and I had to bundle him quickly down the stairs and out of range of our host's hearing.

Music on Land and Sea

During the 1960s and '70s I worked absurdly hard, making a lot of money, or so it seemed to me, but little compared to even a third-rate conductor or soloist. I managed to be in the ECO, the LPO and the Melos all at the same time and to play in freelance concerts and sessions as well. I became a Samaritan volunteer (and was one for the next twenty-five years), sometimes fitting in my sessions of work for them between morning rehearsals and evening concerts at the Festival Hall, going to the Samaritan Centre in the City and giving it my total concentration.

In concerts at the Festival Hall the LPO played with most of the well-known conductors of the time, Sir Georg Solti, for instance. In the 1960s, when I worked with him, he was a very thin, lively, bald man. Johnny called him 'the Screaming Skull' after a horror film of the time, and that name stuck, even when he got fatter. He was one for endless talking, giving orchestras hours of restful day-dreaming. Very good at his own choreography and impressive to watch from the auditorium, he was wonderfully good at presentation and publicity. Very expensive to hire. Popular with audiences, but boring for orchestras, though not aggressive towards them. A highly professional career-musician. As one of the LSO said to me in 1991, "He's an ego-insulated idiot – but a nice man." Unlike most conductors, who become benign in old age, he became irritable and aggressive to players later on and was positively disliked by orchestras, rather than merely put up with as before.

I played often with Raymond Leppard when he conducted the ECO, and also as a duo team with him, when he was the piano or harpsichord accompanist. I enjoyed this enormously. Because he had good musical

Raymond Leppard (Photo RA)

ideas and was more bossy, he, the nominal accompanist, was actually the leader. He was also the leader socially. He was good at getting on with the rich and famous, and he arranged for us to play in their beautiful houses; he said it was professionally correct to be polite and charming to them and thought my left-wing political views sentimental, and we argued about that amiably.

We didn't take our recitals very seriously, but played with jollity and vitality. There is a silly, pretty 'Beethoven' flute sonata, which is probably spurious; in a live broadcast of it, on the spur of the moment we camped it up, putting in silly rubatos and pauses. Raymond quietly giggled while playing the piano, and I, it seemed, spluttered into my flute. I have a recording of the broadcast and there is no sound of sputtering, so I had better self-control than I'd thought.

Later, we did a series of Bach concerts in St John's, Smith Square, which included all the flute sonatas. The BBC recorded them. I wasn't pleased with my playing, for I was starting to be more self-critical, which did no good; my playing lost more from lack of spontaneity than it gained from greater care. During the time of these concerts, Raymond's beautiful early-nineteenth-century house in Hamilton Terrace caught fire and the Steinway upstairs fell through the collapsed floor on to the harpsichord below. His new curtains and decor were destroyed. Firemen saved the stairs and the top-floor bedrooms, but the bedrooms were unusable because of the strong, lingering smell of smoke. Raymond was astonishingly calm about this: no fuss, no complaints, just getting on with rehearsing and playing. Admirable, I thought.

During the next Bach concert after the fire, I smelt burning, so between movements of a sonata, fearing that the hall was on fire and realising that the BBC's microphones were live, I whispered to him nervously, "What's that smell?"

"Yes, I know what it is," he said. "It's my socks; they were in my bedroom during the fire and *they're* giving off the smell."

Again, because of the audience and the microphones, this seemed irresistibly funny.

Just before the war started in Lebanon, the ECO, conducted by Leppard, played there. We travelled by bus through the still-peaceful, green and productive Beka'a valley to Baalbek and played in the huge Roman remains whose rough sculpture seemed to have been carved carelessly by the Romans for this commercial outpost of empire. But it must have impressed the local traders long ago and it impressed me by its absurd grandeur, even now, when ruined. The rich of Beirut drove out to Baalbek for the concerts. As there were many dispossessed Palestinians living near by, security was strong and columns of troops arrived, turning the little town into a barracks. But the ruins were still magical, and playing Malcolm Arnold's First Flute Concerto in the

The ECO rehearsing at Baalbek (Photo RA)

temple of Bacchus under the open, black sky I felt at first misplaced, or mistimed, by sixteen centuries, but when singing out the simple, beautiful tune of the slow movement, the past and present seemed to be linked comfortably; the rich, expatriate Romans might have liked it as much as the rich, 1970s Beirut Lebanese, who had arrived in their air-conditioned Mercedeses, apparently, like the fourth-century Romans, complacent and unaware of coming catastrophe.

A lunch party was given for the orchestra in a grand house in the hills, and some of those prosperous Lebanese also were guests. After admiring the panorama of Beirut and the sea from the terrace, I came into the dining-room and saw servants carving joints of meat; as they carved, they held their heads backwards and sideways, as though the meat stank. I asked a local guest about this, and he explained that our host was Christian and that the meat being served was pork; the servants were Muslims and of course hated having to carve it. The pork was the only food provided and it was the host's deliberate insult to his many Muslim guests, guests who would so soon become his enemies in war.

Raymond made a warm speech thanking our hosts, not knowing until afterwards why we'd eaten that excellent pork.

With his talent for many kinds of music, it is a loss to British music that Raymond went to the USA. More opportunities, more scope, less restriction there, he said; and the USA is central, Europe peripheral. Like Rattle in Birmingham, he took over the orchestra at Indianapolis and made it world class. For a while he seriously considered becoming American, but later decided not to, and stayed on in Indianapolis in his retirement from the orchestra there.

Through Raymond, I met John Betjeman, who was pleasant to have dinner with, not at all pushy or dominating, as famous people often are. He loved my father's paintings and bought six of them after my father died in 1965.

Not knowing him well, I was a little surprised when he asked me to have lunch just with him, and we ate in a restaurant in Smithfield, near where he lived. After general chat and a great deal of wine, he asked me in detail about my sex life and I talked freely. I thought then that this was his only reason for asking me out, and I didn't mind. I liked him. But now, many years later, it seems more probable that he found me unexpectedly dull and so got me to talk on the only subject which would be of interest to both of us – simply good manners. It was reported that, when very old, he said that, although he had had an excellent life, the one thing he regretted was not having had enough sex. This regret was surprising, for he had such a relaxed and positive enjoyment in life, getting pleasure everywhere from everyday things, not needing the luxuries that most people long for.

He would have loathed being a passenger on the soft and effortless luxury of the cruises that the English Chamber Orchestra played on. We went for a fortnight at a time to the West Indies in the winter and the Mediterranean in the summer. For the orchestra, it was sunshine and caviare in a grand hotel with the front door locked, for you can't just walk out of a ship as you can a hotel. One winter we started with a few days' rehearsal in Florida. I wrote about the trip at the time, and here is some of what I wrote.

January 4th. Fort Lauderdale. Almost nothing here but hotels and beeeeeach to infinity. Swam in warm, January water – why the hell do I live in gloomy, grey England instead of in sunshine? Handsome people sunbathing, thin and healthy-looking; but aren't all Americans supposed to be fat? A beach sign said, 'No Solicitors'. Thought for a moment it meant no prostitutes and looked with new curiosity at passing people; it can't mean no lawyers, so I suppose it's actually no hawkers. Overheard a man saying to his woman, "Baby, you're not stoopid. You're too dumb to be stoopid." I really am in America.

January 5th. Rehearsals in the beach-side hotel, where we're staying before joining the ship. Gorgeous Haydn symphony with Pinky Zukerman, the violinist, ineffectually waving a baton (perhaps he hasn't understood that conducting's a job to be learnt, like any other). Then he played, without conductor, a Beethoven romance. It was so touching. Refined, sophisticated, heart-felt; yet he's such a silly, simple man.

A violin virtuoso must start intensive practice at about six years old, missing normal childhood. By the age of ten, he is playing adolescent, sexual music, such as Brahms and Tchaikovsky, caught up in the intense projection of emotions that don't occur to most children till their late teens. Then, people remark, correctly, how old he is for his years. At thirty and older, he must still project these teen-age emotions, which are now too young for an adult, and he seems childish, held back in the adolescent mode of displaying crude emotions. Presumably Pinky was old for his age at ten, and he is certainly childish in his twenties, but he has the personality of a leader. Without being bossy, he takes charge, so those around him become satellites. Not wanting to be his satellite, I keep away. Without apparent effort or affectation, he centres a concert audience on to himself even before he starts to play. A mystery.

This evening, we boarded the ship which will take us through the West Indies as far as Venezuela and back to Florida. Very luxurious. Free drinks at the bar on deck, day and night – well, at least the usual English pay-your-round-or-be-thought-mean won't happen here. The rich passengers, our music customers, look dreadfully dull.

January 6th. A day spent rehearsing in the saloon; gossiping in the sun by the pool with colleagues; drinking; eating. Supper: caviare, vodka; lobster set on fire with brandy, Gewürztraminer to drink with it; little lamb chops with artichoke hearts and asparagus and good claret (can't remember what claret), little goat-cheeses; no sweet – too full.

January 7th. Half an hour of exercises on deck with the rich paunches, organised by a pretty young girl – hard to believe she's the same species as the exercisers. One American lady's so fat that from the rear she seems to have her breasts on backwards, and some of the men look like breasty, topless old women.

January 8th. A few hours at St Thomas in the Virgin Islands, which, seventy years ago, was bought by the USA from Denmark. Pretty, Danish buildings and a vast duty-free shopping area. The hyper-rich passengers scramble greedily for bargains, the poorish orchestra aren't interested.

Played in a beautiful, bare, well-restored Lutheran church. The only audience was the ship's passengers; local faces peered in through the windows. Jean-Pierre Rampal, one of several well-known soloists on board, played a Mozart flute concerto; beautiful, narcissistic Rampal, not Mozart. I know how he feels. It's sexual; there is contact with the audience, like love. He exposes the flute, waving it upwards; look at me! I'm to be loved, to be worshipped. (I dreamt years ago that, instead of carrying my flute on to the platform, I showed off my erect penis.) It's infantile, pulling the musician back from an adulthood that, in my case at least, is being achieved with effort. An adult would exhibit the music, not himself, otherwise he is trapped in childhood. So the virtuoso has two traps; one, the extrovert display of simple emotion, and, two, the sexual display of himself; both traps causing regression to infantilism. Audiences collude with show-off musicians, identifying with their childish sexuality, and many would no longer come to hear a virtuoso who grew up. So a virtuoso's childishness is his livelihood.

Leaving St Thomas this evening, I leant on the rail of the deck in the warm night air and watched as the ship slowly and silently left harbour. The full moon was wide and white on the calm water. We passed the brightly lit Holiday Inn, also reflected on the water, and the cool moonlight mixed its reflection with the yellow electric light. As we quietly moved along, the yellow and white slowly separated out, leaving the glittering moonlight to itself. A colleague was leaning on the rail next to me and we talked gently and sadly of nothing, just the usual gossip, but with a flavour that fitted the scene in front of us. He seemed depressed, but couldn't say so. When depressed, you can't say what you mean, you don't know what you mean, you don't know what you are.

January 9th. Martinique. Sea-sick at night. The ship's French nurse supplied a large pill for it, which, much to my surprise, I had to put up my bum. It cured the sickness rapidly.

Fort-de-France really is France; French shops, bread, restaurants, cemeteries, even French-looking black people. A Gothic-style Cathedral, pretty, delicate, which turns out, when you look at it closely, to be made of cast iron like a ship, the plates bolted together. Earthquake protection?

A good concert. Pleasure and concentrated attention. I have been playing music for so very many years, almost daily enthralled by it, often bored by it, but still have no understanding of how it works. Why does it do what it does? It seems to say something, but what? For instance, there was a simple Mozart minuet this evening, the encore. Its perfection gave me goose-flesh and wet eyes. Why? This was not only caused by the music itself, but also by the silent, intently listening audience, a tribal communion. But music does seem to be saying something very nearly translatable into words, giving information about how things really are, or ought to be, or how much below perfection we are, or what another world is like – but I'll go even further into nonsense if I continue. But if any subject at all is investigated deeply enough, say physics, time, or consciousness itself, at the end there is always to be found the same black sky of mystery. Music isn't the only thing that's mysterious.

If, in an unlikely future, music is explained, it won't be needed any more. Words would then do the job better. But you can't argue against what music says; you can't sensibly say, "No, Beethoven, life's not like how you present it in the fugue at the end of opus 130," except to say vaguely that it expresses optimism and you don't agree with that optimism.

January 10th. Up early. Not sick at all. Passed close by the island of Carriacou, which years ago I went to on holiday, that time on a rolling, heaving schooner. Wow, the sickness (and no bum-pills then). When I was there, I walked away from an empty beach up into the arid, denuded hills (all trees having been used up for schooner-building). A man on the road spoke to me and we chatted. He said that although *he'd* seen a white man before, his wife hadn't, and he took me into his little shack for a jovial, laughing meeting. They gave me a present of ground-nuts (and tried to give me uncooked eggs, which I politely refused), and said what a great day it was for them. Now, Carriacou has luxury hotels and is known as a 'yachtsman's paradise'.

Continuing past Carriacou, we reached St Georges, Grenada. A few of us musicians didn't go on the arranged tour of the island (those tours that make you feel you've seen a place on TV, not really), but wandered off into the little town. It's the only pretty town in the West Indies – French eighteenth-century brick houses and an English early-nineteenth-century parish church overlooking the steep harbour, and also a jolly bus-station-cum-market specialising in the multiple products of the nutmeg tree as well as the multi-coloured buses.

I took four colleagues to the house of a European couple I knew from earlier holiday visits, Beryl and Derrick. Warm welcome from Beryl: kisses, wonderful surprise, come in everyone, have some rum. She soon explained that Derrick is now her ex-husband and lives with a new young wife. After a short discussion with us, some more rum and a phone call to Derrick, she quickly hired a mini-bus. Then Beryl, the five of us and a local driver set off to the south of the island to visit him. After a bumpy, hot, jolly, chatty ride we arrived at Derrick's new house, which was alone by its long crescent of beach. His new wife is Greek, very young and pretty. She seemed delighted to see her husband's first wife and five strangers and gave us rum. A lovely place, with pale, arid vegetation and small hills. Warm sea. No need for swim-suits. Hot sun. Rum. Glad to show my colleagues why I visit the West Indies for holidays. I'm here and now. Heat. The sun. My body is light-weight. We laugh. Rum. There is no past or future. It's all a big, grand now. The sun on the sea.

[Note from the 1990s: since then a huge Cuban-built airport has been built right by Derrick's house and beautiful beach, the airport that was later on invaded by Reagan's USA. I've no news of Derrick and Beryl.]

January 11th. Caracas. All the passengers and musicians went by bus up the steep road from the port to high-up, raucous, rich and slummy Caracas. Traffic-jams and hooting. During the journey, a local woman spoke on the bus's address system, praising Venezuela: rich from oil, world leader in the arts, free education, and, as we passed appalling slums, she explained how the poor were so happy in their shacks that they refused to move out. As we passed mansions, with high walls and barbed wire, with their windows heavily barred against attack, she spoke of the falling crime-rate.

Pleasant concert and meal and then the bus down the long hill, back to the ship; we would have learnt more about Caracas from a half-hour TV documentary than from our rushed visit – but that's tourism.

We cruised on back to Miami and took the plane home.

The ECO also played in Iran just before the Shah was deposed, all seeming relaxed and normal to me. After a concert in Shiraz, some of us took a trip to Darius's ruined city of Persepolis and I took many photographs, being especially impressed with the staircase of statues of kings bearing gifts. I took shots of the kings, carefully avoiding the damaged ones. Half an hour later I was surprised to come across a graffito carved into an ancient pillar which read, 'Rich'd Strachey 1800', so I photographed that too, for until his death I'd known a modern Richard Strachey. On returning to England I took the photograph of the graffito to Esmé, Richard's widow, and we looked at her book of the Strachey family history. There had indeed been an ancestral Richard Strachey who had visited Persia in 1800 and the book described how he had gone to Persepolis and, like me, been impressed with the gift-bearing kings, and, wanting a memento of his visit, had taken a pick-axe to one of them and hacked off its head.

Above: the Strachey graffito at Persepolis (Photo RA)
Below: carvings of kings bearing gifts on the staircase at Persepolis (Photo RA)

Samaritans

In 1964 everything was going well in my life. A pleasant young Londoner called Bryan was living with me, work was less annoying than it had been, money was plentiful and I was enjoying life. Then I started to feel I needed to do something to help the less fortunate – perhaps it was gentle guilt at awareness of my own good fortune.

First I went to the Red Cross and they arranged for me to go each week to see a lonely ninety-five-year-old, a sweet old man called Mr Honey – not a hard task, for he was so interesting. He made tea for us in his tiny, shabby, mews house by Sloane Square, lent to him as 'grace and favour' by his last employers; and, as we drank the tea, I got him to talk about himself. He'd been a manservant in great country houses all his life and he amused me with vivid tales of the strange goings-on in them. In those houses, he explained, everything for the servants was provided – food, lodging and even entertainment – and they were paid almost nothing, being near-slaves. Also, they were, in effect, not allowed to get married, for if they had, they would have been dismissed with no hope of another job; actually, one footman in the house was secretly married to a chambermaid, and, with the compliance of his colleagues, crept silently and fearfully to her bedroom each night. The old man had been a footman when young ("because of my good-shaped calves") and, before waiting at table, had had mutton fat spread on to his hair and flour spooned on top of that in order to imitate a white wig. He didn't complain about this, and the jolly sociability of below-stairs life had been wonderful, he said, and he'd had a perfectly happy life. He died at ninety-six, a year after I first went to see him.

As my do-gooding mood was still influencing me, I went to St Stephen's church in the City, where the Samaritans had their only London premises at the time, in order to ask if I could help with their work. I was interviewed briefly, went to a few lectures about the group, including one by Chad Varah, the organisation's founder, where he was uncommonly outspoken about sex, "in order to scare off any prim Lady-Bountifuls", he told me later.

Nowadays it's quite a business to get accepted as a Samaritan volunteer, but then it was easy. The Samaritans are so different now from then. Now there are many volunteers in each of the many branches in London and around the world, and there is a professional-standard organisation, well-trained office staffs, and clear ideas of how to do the job. Then there was a small, crowded vestry, with two amateur secretaries and two volunteers, plus Chad Varah overseeing, criticising, wrenching the single telephone in the office out of the hand of any volunteer he thought wasn't answering a call in the correct way. Every day the same crazy woman stood in a corner of the room as though put there for being naughty; the same crazy man came in each day and talked to us for hours. The church pews were used for interviewing people who came in needing help.

I gradually learnt what to do and, except when abroad, went on duty about once a week for the next twenty-five years, giving it up on my seventieth birthday for fear of being too old and thus no longer quick-witted enough. I also did what came to be called 'befriending', which is meeting and repeatedly seeing callers away from the Centre to try to help them over a crisis. One difficulty of that was that it had to be made clear at the start that the close and confidential relationship that was about to take place had to end before long, sometimes a hard thing to do without causing pain.

Depressives, the most usual type needing befriending, are often attractive people for a short time, for they have an appealingly low self-image, but they tend to pull you into their depression if you see them too often. You can't argue with a depressive about his state of mind, for it's no more rational to be happy than to be miserable – in fact often rather the reverse. The happy bubble-up of happiness is often the irrational state, not depression, which can be a realistic view of a person's life.

I was often asked, "Why do *you* feel happy? What is the reason for happiness?" And I'd say something like, "There isn't any reason. It's just that when you're in good health, mentally and physically, and even if things aren't going particularly well, misery doesn't happen all that easily. It's how we're made. Something must be wrong for you to be feeling like you do. Let's find out about it." If it seemed likely that the depression was endogenous, not only caused by outside circumstances, then one could talk about the possibility of medical treatment and, "Do please come in and discuss it."

I was often scared when waiting by the phone. Who will the next caller be? A weeping girl who can't say what's wrong? A man whose wife has just left him? A man confessing to sexually molesting his daughter? An Indian woman unhappy in an arranged marriage? Any problem could arrive.

The basic principle of the Samaritans is to be as passive as possible. Don't try to take charge. Don't give advice, for the caller always knows more about him or herself than you do. Get the caller to talk. Let him/her try to find out what is the right thing to do. Give warm sympathy. Get him/her to came into the office to talk face-to-face, if that seems best.

One frequent type of caller is the one who starts by saying, "I'm ringing to ask for advice." You ask a few questions and there is a long conversation; then, much later, the caller ends by saying, "Thank you very much for your help and most valuable advice," when all you've said is "Yes" and "I'm so sorry" and "Tell me more about that". Sometimes I'd get very much involved and need a rest after a long call, but there would always be someone to talk over what had happened, which would calm me down.

Sometimes I must have spent too much time worrying about others, especially about 'befriendees', too many hours at it for my own good, and other people's worries got a bit obsessional. At one of those times a series of misfortunes happened to me (though, oddly I can't remember what they were). I got depressed myself and believed I was being punished by God for trying to take over the sort of work that only He should do. I thought of crucified saints – crucified, I thought then, as punishment for trying to usurp God's job – and believed that I was being slightly put down for my slight uppishness, though not, of course, in the same league as the saints with their huge goodness and huge punishment. I've been in some odd states in my time, and from my present atheistic standpoint this seems very odd indeed. At the time, like the 'Why me' cry of lottery winners, air-crash survivors and cancer sufferers, I was trying to give shape to and explain random happenings, seeing faces in clouds.

Like most of my fellow volunteers, I'd even then get a bit suspicious about my motives for doing this sometimes rather grim work, and we'd talk together about it. On the whole it was decided that motives, unless unusually suspect, weren't relevant if the result was a reduction of suffering. (Really suspect motives such as covert sexual excitement from clients' confessions, a strong wish to run other people's lives, or a tendency to proselytise religion, got prospective volunteers booted out during their training.) But I realised then that my motives were mixed. Working for the Samaritans (or 'the Sams', as volunteers always called it) improved my self-image. It made me think that people admired me for my 'selflessness', and that was pleasing then – and, though the thought makes me squirm a bit now, I'm still today capable of telling people that I was a Samaritan for the same reason. The thought of being admired was, and maybe still is, compensation for my feeling of inferiority at being gay. Also, I should add that helping people sometimes gave me a feeling of power, so different from being told what to do in an orchestra.

What I did understand at last was that the most reliable route to happiness is to be found in being helpful to other people, that helping others is one of the most self-rewarding, thus one of the most selfish, things you can do. The sense of lack, expressed in anguish about lack of success, lack of sex, lack of possessions (all only temporarily relievable), disappears if you spend a lot of time helping people. During later life I only sometimes remember that truth.

I very much enjoyed the companionship of my fellow volunteers while we were working so closely together, and this made me more outward-looking, counteracting my tendency towards inward-looking depression. I can't imagine what it's like even to try to do good over the long term with absolutely pure motives; but I don't think it's wrong to be happy at doing good, any more than it's right to feel happy doing harm.

As for doing good short-term, I thought of my reaction to suffering animals. If I was walking in the country and came across a screaming rabbit in a trap, like most people I'd want to free it. This sudden wish would have nothing to do with my self-image, or being admired. It would be a quick un-thought-out reaction. And I sometimes reacted to Samaritan callers as to a screaming rabbit; I felt I must help, and sometimes the help offered palpably made people less unhappy. Of course, with people, unlike with rabbits, you're on a level footing, person to person, not person to rabbit, and so the involvement was not from above, but a close one between equals.

I was once told, "The Samaritans are a lot of middle-class people who do good works for the lower orders," which made my fellow volunteers laugh when I repeated it to them.

Decline

Although busy with the Samaritans, it was, of course, music and flute-playing that had most of my attention, and from 1961 to '70 music for me mainly meant the LPO.

Bernard Haitink was the principal conductor towards the end of that time. He was a slow developer, and when I first worked with him he was the prototype boring Dutchman; reliable, and uninspiring. Later on, he became more overtly emotional in his music-making and more interesting to work with. Staid-looking and slow, he was apparently the solid family man, yet he allowed his marriage to break up by having a silly love affair; and, apparently always in control of his emotions, he was much upset when, during a rehearsal of Beethoven's Ninth, the second flute-player pointed out a wrong note which he had heard written in the second violin part, which Haitink thought he himself should have noticed, not a player. I don't remember outstanding concerts with him, just good ones; but we all liked him, and over the years we saw how he developed.

In 1970, during a recording with him and the LPO of Holst's Planets, very noisy music, the sounds in my ears became distorted, so a few days later I visited a Harley Street ear-specialist.

After examination and testing, he said, as far as I remember, "You've had a lifetime of work in orchestras. From your ears' point of view, that's very hazardous. You know, some musicians' ears stand up to this without damage, others don't, and you'll just have to accept that you're one of the unlucky ones. I'm afraid the damage to the nerves is irreversible."

So I left the LPO and played for a time in quiet music, whenever it was possible to choose it, using ear-plugs if it got loud, even in concerts.

Bernard Haitink (centre) with the LPO in Japan (Photo RA)

I heard myself and others playing, but the sound, with or without earplugs, was a distorted buzz so, of course, my playing was poor; but I got away with it most of the time because of long experience and by taking extra care. But there was no joy in playing.

Each night in bed I put my mechanical watch to each ear to see how much ticking was audible. At first, the right ear heard nothing, the left just a little, then, after a few weeks, a dull, top-filtered sound; and finally, after many months, both ears heard the watch normally. After a year or so, my hearing was all right again. The specialist had been wrong. (Now, in my eighties, I still hear well.) But it was a depressing year, waiting to see if I'd come to the end of my flute-playing.

I still worked hard. In my diary for November 1971, I see recorded the following places where I played with the ECO on consecutive days: Paris Nuremberg Munich Frankfurt Wuppertal Dusseldorf Zurich Biel Lausanne Basle Geneva Schaffhausen Strasbourg Paris. A nightmare, leaving no memory. In Germany and the United States, concert tours are promoted with such efficiency, using every moment of expensive orchestras' time, that all the players do each day is to eat travel eat play drink sleep; eat travel eat play drink sleep; eat travel eat play drink sleep; eat travel – and so on for several weeks.

In 1972, there was another ECO tour, but this one I remember. The places, properly spaced out with rest-days, were: Salvador-Bahia, Rio, Brasilia, São Paulo, Curitiba, Porto-Allegre, Montevideo, Buenos Aires, Cordoba, Santiago, Lima, Caracas, Bogotá, Panama, Managua, Mexico City, Merida and Kingston (Jamaica). John Pritchard was conducting on this trip and he was the perfect touring conductor, relaxed and lazy when the going was rough, but sufficiently in control when necessary. The tour was organised by Ursula Jones, a cultured and energetic Swiss woman, who believed (unlike most tour organisers) that orchestras should have time off to relax and sightsee. From Lima there was time, for those of the orchestra who wanted to, to go by air up to Cuzco and then on by bus to a little Indian town with its market. It was so enthralling that I totally ignored frequent vomiting caused by altitude sickness, only later going to bed and taking whiffs of oxygen, supplied routinely by the Cuzco hotel.

In Nicaragua we drove by jeep high up in the mountains and looked into a vast volcano, and in Yucatan visited vast Mayan remains. Those players who disliked sightseeing spent disgruntled days in hotel bars complaining that they made less money because of doing fewer concerts.

We visited Caracas, Bogotá and Panama in three consecutive days. In Caracas I was damn nearly mugged, but was saved by the chance arrival of a police car, the thugs then running away; my pocket was picked by a gang in a main street in Bogotà; and in Panama City I was attacked and robbed by a large mob of teenagers – and all that was taken from me in the three incidents was a small Spanish-English dictionary, ten dollars and a valueless watch. Isn't it odd that the only times (three so far) this has happened to me were all in the space of those three consecutive days.

After the last concert of the tour, in Jamaica, John Pritchard and I both stayed on there for holidays in different parts of the island. For the weekend, I went with the friends I was staying with to their remote country house, an old wooden building on a large estate which in the past had produced peppery allspice (called pimento in Jamaica). It was so beautiful and peaceful, with its long view from the balcony down over trees to the distant sea, that, when my friends returned to Kingston, I stayed on, alone, for the week until they returned for another party the next weekend. The first peaceful day was wonderful, especially after the long hours of travel, the many concerts in South America and the recent noisy bustle of friends. During the lonely night in the shabby wooden house I was scared, scared of the dark and scared of imagined, ghostly previous occupants who seemed to be creeping about and creaking the floor boards. I noted where the matches were so that I could quickly light a candle, and locked the bedroom door, which is not a very rational way of keeping out ghosts, but it made me feel better.

After that disturbed night, when, half disappointingly, no ghost appeared, I had breakfast and then idly looked around the many outhouses in the yard and came across a large metal trunk, which I opened. Inside it were diaries showing that previous occupants of the house had for generations been English vicars of the local parish church. Trips to England were mentioned, especially for a son who'd been educated at Tonbridge School. That night, I slept well. There were many English clerics in my family, so I felt that the ghosts must be friendly.

Later in the week, I left the old house for two days in order to visit John Pritchard, driving in an appalling old hired Morris Minor along the north coast road to where he was staying, near Montego Bay. He was in luxury. There was a Hollywood-type house, a pool, a new Chevrolet with chauffeur, and food and drink laid on by diffident and stand-offish servants. Fat, hot John spent his time drinking gin and tonic, brought to his lounging chair under an umbrella by the pool, and he seemed bored and depressed. I sat with him and was waited on too. I'm humiliated by servants, wanting to shout, "Look, I'm human, and just as good as you. Stop sneering and standing apart." As an orchestral musician, a servant myself, I know how they feel; but as a conductor, John didn't. His companions were two New York gays he seemed not to like much, and nor did I; he hated swimming and sunshine and didn't seem to be interested in Jamaica. I failed to cheer him up and was glad to go back to the shabby old wooden house in the hills.

On returning to London after travelling, I find people don't now want to hear about far-off places; there is enough of that on television. We don't want to listen and be diverted from our own worlds, unless there's unusually tasty gossip about a trip, so my photographs of that trip remained largely unseen.

The English Chamber Orchestra, with which I went to South America and Jamaica, is different from all the other orchestras in London in that it's run by a single man (for Ursula Jones gave up her directorship of it long ago and took a degree and a PhD in pre-Columbian archaeology, her interest in the subject stimulated by those trips with the ECO). Unlike the symphony orchestras, the ECO has no elected board of players to run it or to advise the management; instead, it has a director, Quintin Ballardie, who also plays principal viola in it. He and Ursula built up the orchestra brilliantly and he continues to run it on his own.

Ballardie engaged Simon Rattle to conduct the ECO in Barcelona when Rattle was a young boy, a quite unknown deputy, engaged at the last moment, and we were all impressed by his musical gift and good manners. Years later, with the Philharmonia, I found that he still treated orchestras as people, not as keyboards to be played, and the orchestra thought his conducting of Rachmaninov's Second Symphony, which we played with him then, was adequate, if not all that inspiring, and we

Simon Rattle (Photo RA)

liked him. He is probably best with his own players and in less crudely romantic music. I hope he hasn't succumbed to the recent absurdly flattering media reports on him and doesn't think that now he's a super-person. When he was rehearsing the ECO in about 1985, I photographed him at work. He was scornful when I showed him the resulting prints (one of which is in this book). "Typical photographer's false idea of the hysterical conductor," he said.

Ballardie also got Murray Perahia to play and conduct Mozart with the ECO. A fine pianist and a super-perfectionist; but as he's never happy with his own or others' playing, he's difficult to work with. Playing in

Murray Perahia (Photo RA)

Mozart piano concertos with him, I was past my best and I expect he was right to pick on me for endless criticism, but I did find this tiresome. In recording with an orchestra, he spoilt the flow of the music by carping on tiny points, so that the music died and his anxiety made tentative music. A likeable, gloomy man, and I'm sorry I didn't play better for him.

Riccardo Muti, with whom I played often in the Philharmonia, was not likeable. Of plebeian origin, but with right-wing politics, he looks good on stage, but is musically dull and an arrogant, coarse bully; I haven't met a player with a good word to say for him, as he makes all those he works with feel inadequate and unhappy. Conducting and politics can attract the same type, the power-hungry and the vain; they can succeed in their careers, but they cause unhappiness all around.

Claudio Abbado also looks good on stage and is an arrogant, smooth bully. Of patrician origin, but with left-wing politics, he is wonderfully charismatic in music he has conducted often. He is polite and charming to his players; but that is only skin deep, and he was hated by the LSO when he was their principal conductor. As well as hating him, they complained that he used Youth orchestras for learning new repertory, played it in concerts with the LSO and then, when at last he knew it well, recorded it (the best-paid work) in America, thus making the LSO seem of only middling status. In 1983, I went to the USA with him and the LSO and they played badly, especially in the bigger cities. Because of Abbado's contemptuous attitude, they lost self-confidence, though that is what they are renowned for at home. The quiet music in Mahler's First Symphony became unplayable because of his grimaces and gestures and his insistence that they played it more quietly than is possible. The result was sour tuning and cracked notes from the wind. Because of panic, an excellent wind player failed in every performance to play one easy, quiet, solo note in the Mahler symphony, the last note of a movement, so that the movement seemed to fail to end. It was sad to hear formerly tip-top (and conceited) players reduced to student level in front of discerning American audiences.

Abbado disliked the way I played; for instance, he politely asked me to play without vibrato, then, when I did so, said that the cold sound was unpleasant. He got my co-principal to play in my place and I was relegated to a subsidiary position; as he is an experienced and discriminating musician I took his criticism to heart and became depressed. I was sixty-three and had noticed how old wind- and string-players have trouble with vibrato and tone-quality, both of which he was criticising in my playing. When using vibrato, they have reduced sensitivity to very small changes in pitch; their own vibrato sounds to them less wide than it used to, so they widen it. As to tone-quality, they have reduced sensitivity to high frequencies, so they hear themselves as too dull and thus brighten their sound into harshness. Although aware of these hazards, I'd apparently failed to avoid them. We were playing in Tokyo then, and I was distressingly given a lot of time off work because of Abbado's dislike of my playing, but this was made easier because of my good luck in knowing someone who lived there.

I'd met Vincent Wong, a Chinese, in Jakarta some years earlier when he was working in the Singapore Embassy there, and I got to know him better when he was with the Singapore High Commission in London later on. He is open and friendly, the opposite of the inscrutable oriental of nineteenth-century fiction. He wasn't a close friend, just an acquaintance who was by chance often working in eastern places I happened to visit. In Jakarta, he'd kindly shown me what it was like living in that hot, crowded, dangerous city; and as he was working in Tokyo at the time of my visit, he showed me around entertainingly, happy to have someone to be with. He was lonely and I was delighted to be with him in my unhappy time off from playing and to visit him in his large, quiet flat, a great luxury in crowded Tokyo. Vincent's face is a parody of the European's idea of an Easterner, slit-eyed and sallow, and the Japanese first thought he was one of them; but he spoke their language only haltingly and, when this was heard, he was thought to be Korean. The Japanese are polite to Westerners but contemptuous and abusive to Koreans, and not much better to Chinese, which was why he was lonely and unhappy and pleased to be with a non-Japanese.

For my entertainment, on a day when I was at a loose end, but he was working, he suggested that I go by myself out of Tokyo to Nikko, a group of shrines, about seventy miles to the north. He told me how to get to the railway station, how to buy the ticket, the exact cost of it, which platform to go to and how to know where to get off the train (the station names being in Japanese script). So I set off without difficulty in the comfortable, slow train, not a Bullet, going first through the huge city and then on the long, straight track through flat land with little fields and little, square, red houses, which reminded me of my first journey to Paris so long ago.

Nikko was a disappointment. There are magnificent temples there; but the crowds, the mobs of children, each with their teacher shouting into a loud-hailer, and the air of commerce, made me feel even worse than I'd felt in Tokyo. Unlike the journey nearly all the way there, Nikko is in the hills and I could see peaceful-looking woods all around, so I took a path away from the tourism and noise and set off for a quiet walk. The path curled upwards through the trees, over the hilltop away into silence and into a replica of a Japanese print, with absurdly steep hillsides covered with orderly pine trees. After a time, and still high up, I came to a quiet and deserted temple, so different from the commercialised Nikko ones, and sat there calmly and alone for a couple of hours, regaining sanity after not only Nikko but also after Abbado and my loss of self-esteem. In this sacred place I attained a detached overview, seeing the pettiness of the problem, and returned to Tokyo strengthened; then, a few days later, continued the tour to Australia and on around the world in a more cheerful and accepting mood. But realising that I needed a sense of self-worth in order to be happy was puzzling and irritating, and it seemed childish that I couldn't be aware of my own mediocrity and still be OK. Yes, irritating; but I suppose we *all* need this absurd, irrational self-esteem.

But on returning to England, again I was depressed and lost confidence in my playing, then slowly rediscovered what I'd first found in the shrine near Nikko, that in old age my self-esteem was no longer only about my flute-playing, as it had been when young, but was now more widely based and that I valued myself for other qualities as well. After spending more than sixty years in childhood and adolescence, I was slowly becoming an adult; what would have been a big humiliation in youth could now be seen as just one small incident in a long and immensely enjoyable career; I was able to accept slowly giving up playing and gradually being offered less interesting work. I also accepted without annoyance that my flute-playing colleagues and rivals would hear about, and spread around, the story of my rejection by Abbado and that it would be linked to my old age and deterioration – after all,

Vincent Wong
(Photo RA)

The peaceful temple near Nikko (Photo RA)

I'd have done the same to old rivals when I was young. Probably because of my reduced status, some fixers stopped giving me their work, and I played gradually less and less during the next seven years until deciding, at seventy, to stop altogether. Apart from the Abbado incident, the ending of my musical career caused no distress, for other interests took over, friendships strengthened because of having more leisure, and life continued on the whole happily.

Last Chapter

In writing this book I've cut a path through the thick jungle of memories, but this path isn't the only one I could have made; I could retrace my steps through that jungle, start again and take a different route. Instead of concentrating on music and musicians, I could, for instance, have written a book about long-term relationships. I've written briefly and only superficially about my parents, and about my sister hardly at all. She and I were close but wary, and the relationship was solid. A lot could have been written about that. As with many siblings, my sister and I were rivals. An account of our early, and in my sister's case life-long, rivalry might possibly have made an interesting, if gloomy, book. But that book would have been far too difficult to write by an amateur author such as myself.

Then there's my aunt, Doff. We loved each other, even to the extent that sometimes I preferred her to my mother and sometimes believed that she loved me even more than her own children.

She was remarkable. After bringing up six children, she learned about eyes, and then became one of Britain's top ophthalmologists, with a practice in Harley Street and also at Moorfields Hospital. She was, I thought, a little cool in manner compared to Noël, my mother, but hugely generous and kind to all around her. She died at the age of ninety-eight, missed and mourned by me and innumerable others.

I could also write about Barron. She was actually *Phyllis* Barron, but it would have been ludicrous to call such a masculine person by so feminine a name. She was, onward from their student days together at the Slade, Noël's closest friend and a sort of godmother to me ('sort of',

Charlotte and her son, Piers (Photo RA)

for I wasn't christened). When Barron died in old age in 1964, I helped Noël, who was an executor of her will, go through and clear out the contents of her desk. During this clearing out I came across what was plainly a long ago love-letter from Noël to Barron – 'Darling Barron, you are the person I shall love for ever…' and then the letter was snatched away.

When I was born there were three adults living in our house; Bernard (my father), Noël – and Barron. I wonder if Bernard unwittingly became part of a *ménage-à-trois*.

Barron lived in the house for eight years, and then moved out to live with her new 'wife', Dorothy. They lived happily together until Dorothy died forty or so years later.

But I think that the sort of book that would have come from my purely personal memories would after all have been a standard account of any old life, in fact just plain boring and not worth the long effort of

*My aunt Doff
(Photo RA)*

Barron (Photo RA)

writing it. All lives, like mine, have their individual oddities, and most are not worth relating; whereas what I've written may be of interest at least to those few people who want to read gossip about long-dead musicians.

I've had a lucky life – or maybe I pick from the memory jungle only the lucky bits. But I *really* have been lucky with money. When young and winning at cards, I used to think of the saying, 'Lucky in money, unlucky in love' (though now I see that I've been lucky in both, for, after all, sex, sexual love and consequent friendships have been major contributors to a richly experienced life).

Yes, lucky in money. I never had a written contract with an orchestra – since London orchestras, except for the BBC Symphony, always worked on just verbal offers and acceptances – and I was also sometimes a freelance; so work produced no automatic pension. I neither put money away for retirement nor saved for a private pension, not thinking about the future, spending my money either at once or on long holidays away from Europe. But in the 1950s I did have the sense to save enough over a few years to buy a pleasant house in the then slummy Notting Hill for £3,000 (which, by coincidence, was what I earned that year). Notting Hill later became an expensive part of London, the house became valuable and it gives me a good living from renting part of it, and also from selling part of the freehold value. A very lucky buy. So far so good, and not only about money, but life generally – though, of course, anything could happen, good, catastrophic or just plain boring; for the world isn't stationary, it throws us about.

But it's all very well my saying that I've reached this lovely, placid, all-forgiving, geriatric plateau, lucky about money and mentally relaxed; but now and then I still slip off it into a prickly thicket of anxiety and depression – but not often. When I'm in that thicket I see myself as a silly old fart doddering about uselessly, just waiting for death; then, probably because of a change in my brain chemistry, everything returns to being pleasant and enjoyable. This relaxed state of mind is in part, I think, caused by being no longer stressed about being gay.

Years ago, I talked to my long-time colleague, the violinist Maggie Cowen, about 'coming out' as a gay man. This conversation was when I was in my fifties, and soon after arriving in Wellington, New Zealand – I'm always garrulous after long flights.

"I prefer," I said, "being laughed at, to my face or behind my back (or even being thought disgusting), to living a secretive life. If I've got to choose between being seen by some people as comical or disgusting, or have to tell lies all the time, I'll choose the former." I didn't see gayness as comic-disgusting, of course, but knew what the opinion of the ignorant was; for instance, I was thinking of tabloid headlines in those days making out gays to be funny freaks (and they still do, for that matter).

My policy worked out all right. For instance, I took a disastrous long-time lover with me for a fortnight to the Aix-en-Provence Festival: Mozart with the English Chamber Orchestra. He liked marijuana and, when he switched from English pot to Provençal hashish, went alarmingly psychotic, poor chap, became incoherent and threatened me with violence; so, when he got a bit better, I put him on to a train from Marseille back to England. This must have produced jolly gossip in the orchestra, but nobody was unpleasant to me about it, or even stopped being friendly. Perhaps we're comfortable with people like me who are considered comical; we're no threat. We're certainly not envious of them as we can be of others more successful than we are in the way they run their lives or their careers, and envy is a life-long vice of many musicians.

When I was young I used to be envious of successful, older, richer musicians, and I've seen some old ones get resentful of younger ones. For instance, when I was middle-aged, I met John Francis (who'd taught me when I was fifteen) in the BBC studios at Maida Vale where I'd been broadcasting some chamber music. At that time he was at the end of a long career, and I was very busy.

I asked him politely what music he was broadcasting, saying, "What are you *doing* here?" and at once realised the ambiguity; for what he heard was a scornful, "What are *you* doing here?" So he replied indignantly, "Aren't I allowed to play for the BBC any more?"

I hope I've avoided getting into that state of mind after the warning sign from Abbado, and I'm surprised to find that the short time between retirement and decrepitude is so very enjoyable. But nowadays, when people say I look fit, I'm reminded of the old saying, 'There are three ages of man: youth; middle age; and "you're looking so well"'; the last said with an intonation of surprise.

I was sixty-nine when I last played in a concert as soloist. This was in Singapore with Marisa Robles, the Spanish harpist, where we went to play Mozart's Flute and Harp Concerto, technically easy for the flute-player. No worry. The main reason I went was that the concerts paid for a holiday in Penang afterwards (with Vincent as my guide and companion, as usual in the East, for he then happened to be working in nearby Kuala Lumpur).

Marisa is a great personality on stage, and in the first of our two identical concerts she quite overshadowed me. I was told that I'd played well, but that all eyes were on her, and the next day the newspaper said I lacked personality. So, in the second performance, I moved about a lot when playing, twinkled at Marisa through her harp-strings, grinned at the conductor during bars' rest, leant sideways towards the violins when in unison with them and generally fooled about. Afterwards there were queues of autograph-hunters waiting for me outside; and later I was told that I had great personality, that I looked so natural and relaxed on the platform and that I'd quite put Marisa in the shade.

Some years before, I did a similar thing. During a televised performance of Tchaikovsky's Pathetic Symphony in the Albert Hall I amused myself by waving the flute up and down when playing, never sitting still, for I was curious about the effect this would have. Several people I knew who saw the broadcast told me they hadn't realised before what a prominent flute part that symphony has (it hasn't, in fact) and how much they liked my outstanding personality.

Possibly, if I'd cynically behaved like that when young, I might have had more success as a soloist, but I'm glad I didn't, for it wouldn't have been natural to me, as it is for the ebullient James Galway, for instance. Anyway, I've been happy working in groups, and only sometimes as a soloist, rather than plodding repeatedly through the small solo flute repertory, a fate that is probably even more tedious in repetition than playing in orchestras has sometimes been; and in solo playing there aren't the pleasures of rapport and equality. But that's not how I felt when young, for then I was full of ambition; and, looking back to my childhood, I think also about the three things I decided that I most wanted from life then.

The first was that I should be the best flute-player in the world.

I failed there; but often I've experienced strongly a *feeling* of success and fulfilment, so perhaps the failure didn't matter.

The second was to have lots and lots of sex.

Success here way beyond adolescent fantasy. Plentiful, blissful enjoyment, combined then with times of strong feelings of guilt and shame (though nowadays it all seems to have been harmless enough). Maybe some people will tut-tut here and say that lots of sexual enjoyment is inferior to a long and devoted marriage, and I won't argue, for they're right – in some cases; but I'll just repeat that for me the sex was indeed blissful.

And the third teenage need was to understand the world.

Failure here, of course. But, all the same, I now have a little knowledge – knowledge beyond me in adolescence – of where the vast areas of my failure of understanding lie. I now understand a bit about the extent of my ignorance.

So, in old age, I can tell the young boy still in me that he was going to be a lucky person, a person who did at least *try* – and ask him to pardon the failures and to revel in the successes.

On retirement at 70 I sold all my flutes, for I feared becoming an incompetent amateur sadly harking back to lost expertise, and I still feel no pangs of regret at the ending of fifty years of professional playing. Before those fifty years began – in 1939, at the start of the war, aged nineteen – I was of course worried about what was to come, and reacted to the worry by managing to live each moment happily without thought for the future; for there was nothing I could do to avoid almost certain future horrors. Now, in old age, I feel like that again, though for different reasons. At the time of writing this I'm healthy, sane and enjoying life, as though again having a holiday as a consolation for future horrors. Will it be almost sudden death from a heart attack (with just a short time of agony and panic), or dementia, or a stroke causing loss of movement and speech, or cancer, or a slow deterioration to a fading out of consciousness? It must soon be one of those or something similar, so let's drink and be merry.

If I could time-travel back to when I was eighteen, when the head of the Royal College, and my flute teacher, and the South Kensington busker *all* said that I wouldn't make a living, I would say to them, "You are wrong. I will make a perfectly good living; and, as well as the usual happiness and misery of being human, I'll have a gorgeous and fulfilling life playing the flute."

Index